I0212330

Praise For *The Future Poor*

In this innovative book, Jonathan Grimm offers what is indeed a grim warning about the looming breakdown of the social contract when it comes to meeting the needs of the elderly. He demonstrates, with vivid detail, that the vast majority of Americans have not been able to make adequate provision for retirement. That is why they are, in fact, The Future Poor. He offers searching analysis of the many things that have gone wrong to get us to this place. And he offers suggestions for ways forward. This book combines both financial acumen and deep Christian moral concern. Highly recommended!

David P. Gushee, Christian ethicist and author of *Changing Our Mind*

Jonathan Grimm paints a picture of a society ill-prepared for the future because the present pillars of contentment are crumbling. His proposal draws upon ancient sources of wellbeing and modern realities of financial systems to prescribe a disciplined path to personal and communal health that includes but transcends financial success. This book is a primer for individuals, families, religious organizations, schools, government, and corporations. It will take rebalancing all communal institutions, not just a portfolio, to create true social security for all of us.

George A. Mason, founder of Faith Commons and author of *The Word Made Fresh*

Jonathan Grimm provides a timely and poignant reminder of the need to step into our power as investors. This book is a must-read for any person evaluating their financial position amidst the economic uncertainty of our times.

Andrea Longton, CFA and author of *The Social Justice Investor*

The Future Poor

How families and communities can join
together to survive the looming retirement crisis

Jonathan Grimm

For more information and further discussion, visit

TheFuturePoor.com

Copyright © 2025 by Jonathan Grimm

Author photo by Alex Scott. ByAlexScott.com

All Rights Reserved
ISBN: 978-1-64180-204-8
Version 1.0

Cover design by Rick Nease
Published by Read the Spirit, an imprint of
Front Edge Publishing
42807 Ford Road
Canton, MI
48187

Front Edge Publishing books are available for discount bulk purchases for events, corporate use and small groups. Special editions, including books with corporate logos, personalized covers and customized interiors are available for purchase. For more information, contact Front Edge Publishing at info@FrontEdgePublishing.com

For Aimee, the first person to see me
and to see what no one else had seen before.
That has been a gift of freedom that I am continuing to learn to live in.
All you have done with me and for me cannot be measured.
This book does not exist without you,
even though I am pretty sure you haven't read it.
I look forward to how we will change the world next.

For Sis, D, and Jimmy,
You three mean the world to me.
Each of you possess such kindness, creativity, and hope.
Daily you remind me that this is a good world
and worth our every effort to keep it that way.

Contents

Up in Flames

What do we do if everything we've worked for suddenly goes up in flames?

We hope that someone will help us to rebuild our lives.

In two sentences, that's the hard-earned wisdom you'll find in this book. I know a good deal about this because, on the verge of finishing this book, my family and I experienced that kind of life-threatening disaster. My wife, our children and I lost our modest California home—and our entire neighborhood—without warning in a raging wildfire.

So with that kind of jolt on the first page, I want to also reassure you from the start: This ultimately is a hopeful book with practical advice that now has been strengthened by my own experiences with my family.

I wrote this book because, both professionally and personally, I am convinced that we can prevent an even larger disaster—the collapse of our nation's retirement system—if we collectively take time to remember and reclaim some of our core community values. Now, that startling statement also may stop you cold. How can that possibly be true? How could a looming retirement crisis be more devastating than rampant wildfires or other natural disasters? Social Security is sacrosanct, isn't it?

Well, my case is far stronger now that we are publishing this book in mid-2025. Now, the evidence of deep flaws in our retirement system is becoming ever more obvious. National headlines are reporting on efforts to overhaul the pillars of our retirement system—even the seemingly untouchable Social Security Administration. What's even more frightening, though, is that this crisis is likely to most fully impact Americans who currently are under age 50 and are earning less than $150,000—in other words: Millions of relatively young people—like our families and friends. What's at stake for those people we know and love? Rather than assuming that they can sail smoothly into retirement years, they are likely to fall below the poverty level. Their visions of "home" could go up in smoke.

That brings me back to our fire.

Just before the publication of this book, my family's home—and everything we couldn't quickly cram into our car that night—was destroyed in a devastating wildfire. Overnight, my whole community—my kids' neighborhood—was gone! That was literally a crash course in the trauma that cascades from such a catastrophic loss.

When I say "catastrophic"—I'm talking about blazing embers, some of which were as big as basketballs, blowing off the mountain behind our neighborhood in 80 mph winds like something out of an alien invasion movie. My son thought of it like a fire breathing dragon descending upon us.

How did that fire catch us almost unawares? The background is that we've lived with fires in this part of the country for years. When this one hit us in early January 2025, we were just a couple days off of a new-year holiday break. Two distinct wildfires broke out on opposite sides of the greater Los Angeles area. The first started in a place called the Palisades right near the Pacific Ocean. The second—the one that nearly engulfed me and my family—was the Eaton Fire that started in Eaton Canyon in the Pasadena/Altadena area near the foothills of LA.

Even that fire, not far from our home, didn't worry us too much as we went to bed that night. There weren't even any evacuation warnings for our area. In the almost twenty years we have lived in Altadena, we have seen several wildfires. In fact, about every four to five years a fire would start up on the mountain but never posed a threat to those of us who live there. Residents who have lived there longer share the same story.

Those earlier fires had never been accompanied by tornado-class winds, which complicated this particular fire to an unimaginable degree. My wife and I put our kids to bed that night and then went to sleep ourselves without any warning from public officials in our region. Fortunately, we woke up at 1:30 a.m. to howling sounds of fire coming for us.

Things changed that day for all of us—and for so many people in one of the world's most influential cities.

In my family we have begun talking about pre-fire and post-fire realities. The bulk of this book—including all of the financial analysis about the deep cracks in our retirement planning—was written by "pre-fire Jonathan." This introductory chapter—and the urgency with which I'm going to be reporting on these issues through my ongoing speaking, teaching, columns and pod-casts—is definitely "post-fire Jonathan."

What unites the vision of pre- and post-fire Jonathan is my life-long sense of the value of community. Even in the coldly, carefully calculated conclusions of my pre-fire research, I kept returning to a profound sense that we must collectively realize that our financial futures are bound up in our communities.

I know what you're thinking: That sounds like a really good idea!

Thanks! I believe it's a good idea too!

But I know you're also thinking: A really good—but hopelessly impractical—idea.

Aren't you curious how I can make this case in a convincing way?

What these wildfires showed me was countless examples of what community collaboration truly does look like. I have experienced it first-hand and believe it to be more powerful than I did in my pre-fire days. I was provided with one of the most vivid and extreme examples of community finance imaginable. Everything from FEMA, friends, family neighbors, churches, non-profits, schools, insurance, local government, and so many more sprang into action to get shelter, food, basics, and everything else.

Parking lots turned into supply distribution for bottled water, diapers, and clothes. Emergency organizations were handing out gift cards. Many friends of those of us that lost everything started GoFundMe pages. People we didn't know began sending donations without hesitation. Stores offered deep discounts or donations for plates and silverware—the basics of life that you don't really think about until you have no home and no place to eat.

Friends and family invited the displaced into their homes. Complete strangers offered hugs while shopping at Target because the obligatory "Sorry for your loss" sounded so empty.

We are often at our best as people in the face of a crisis. We are resilient and we rally. What about a looming crisis like retirement?

There are several lessons that this situation has taught me. And I believe they parallel the message you will discover in the coming chapters.

We don't build a life in a day

Only in the worst of circumstances do we ever start from scratch. The majority of us are born into some sort of existing home where loving folks cares for our basic needs. Especially if you're the "first born"—your family probably also got a lot of outside help when you arrived. News of a pregnancy prompts a baby shower so that new parents and their new baby can have a jump start in this new chapter.

If you are a parent, like me, you know—and are forever thankful for—this reality. When we had our first child—we got all kinds of stuff! Those who had gone before us offered advice and shared with us things that proved most valuable. By the third child—and my wife and I have three—then you're likely transitioning from the grateful receiver of all this wisdom and generosity to becoming the wise organizers of future showers.

The majority of us are fortunate enough to know that the arrival of a baby is truly a team sport. If you're part of a congregation, a community nonprofit or our healthcare network—you know that helping new moms and dads is one of the highest priorities in our communities.

We don't build a life in a day.

We see this same type of community support arising around other milestones of life. When kids graduate high school and go off to college, we provide gifts and jumpstart adulthood with dorm room supplies.

Think of weddings! When a young couple starts out, we love to give them money, knives, blenders, blankets, cups. We even demand that the couple to tell us exactly what they think they need on a registry.

Think of other milestones. How about "housewarming" parties? "Retirement" parties? Thousands of congregations nationwide have ministries to reach out and provide meals when a family is struggling with cancer or a death in the family.

Why is all of this such a deeply rooted part of family life in communities nationwide? Because we all know that we can't build a new life—or rebuild a shattered life—in an instant. It's overwhelming.

And now my family and I are forever grateful recipients of that community impulse to help each other. Our lives were put on pause until some sort of housing was secure. Many of our neighbors were funneled into FEMA hotels or other lodgings.

Was this "shelter"—one of the most basic human needs? Yes.

Were these temporary digs "stability"? Not really.

Were these places we stayed "home"? Far from it!

Some went from a home they had lived in for decades to an empty one-bedroom apartment. Securing something more permanent was certainly a relief and felt like many people's top priority. But pause to consider for a moment the very basic level on which we were struggling—finding shelter. Starting over—from scratch.

I am a fan of thought experiments, as you will come to find out by reading more of this book. Imagine for a moment that you are at "home." Look around at everything that fills the space. From the largest of furniture pieces to the extra set of bed sheets in the closet. Think of all the cans, boxes, and bags in your kitchen pantry—and all the dishes, utensils, and other gizmos in your cupboards and drawers. Think of all the clothes, shoes and accessories in your closets, your dressers, your storage spaces?

How would you replace all of what you see tomorrow? Think of the logistics, the timing, the expense.

It's an overwhelming task to accomplish alone! But, it becomes more possible with more people helping us all along the way.

We need our social pillars

In coming chapters, I will explain why our collective trust in our social pillars is pretty low these days. The data continues to be overwhelming that our belief in government, corporations, faith communities, education, and family is not what it was in decades past—and that's a collective tragedy right now as we face so many challenges.

And yes: I know. I know.

It's easier to encourage us all to renew our trust in these pillars than it is to actually make those pillars operate as solid supports for our communities. Even the role of government in relation to these wildfires—and other ongoing natural disasters—is a matter of debate. Was the government prepared? Did our leaders respond correctly? Did the recovery efforts suffice—or, in some ways, did they make things worse? In this book, you will find that I'm not interested in choosing political sides or blaming one group over another. I wrote this book to voice an inspiring, encouraging call for us to remember that we need to solve our looming problems—*together*.

So, yes, government will continue to be one of the pillars. My constructive appeal to you in this book is energized by my own first-hand experience with the limits and roles of these social pillars in our lives. At the end of the day, we must have a level of government support to build—or rebuild—our individual lives, our communities, and the many institutions we need in our broader society. My constructive appeal to you in this book is energized by my own first-hand experience with the limits and roles of these social pillars in our lives.

That includes the other social pillars as well, including corporations, or at least the good will of their employees. Whatever biases you may have when thinking about the idea of corporations as a pillar—I can tell you that my wife, my kids and I are grateful that they gave us discounts, donations, supplies, goods, and services. Furniture stores gave out mattresses. Clothing stores gave pants. Shoes were half off. Therapists offered therapy. I am sure there was an economic boom as thousands of people immediately had to replace everything. Demand outpaced supply. And while there was a level of profiteering primarily in the housing/rental market, the overall response was positive and supportive for those rebuilding.

Some four hundred school district employees and countless children lost everything in our area. Several schools were lost. Holiday break ended up extended for obvious reasons and yet there was a move to return students in a safe way back to school as soon as possible. Relocating entire schools of children has been a titanic task! Yet, what we have seen so vividly is that all of us understood the value of rebuilding our educational system.

Some of the most beautiful examples of help came from non-profits, faith communities, family, and friends as those pillars all stepped up to the enormous human needs in the wake of these fires.

We need each other

Those of us who lived through this fire season can give first-hand testimony to these hopeful and healthy resources—as scattered and chaotic and sometimes confusing as many of these efforts were as they first roared to life around us.

But, bottom line: My family and I are living proof that we need each other.

And we can share our lives and resources in ways that lift all of us, even in the midst of almost unimaginable trauma.

As I was finishing all the other chapters in this book and my publishing house was preparing this book for final release, I remember thinking to myself: I've found lots of great examples of how my proposal for more cooperative sharing of resources can work—and I've sprinkled them through this manuscript—but I wish I could find one illustration so powerful that it would stop everyone and make us think with renewed energy about these proposals.

What could illustrate this book's central message of hope in the face of looming tragedy?

Now, I am shaking my head. I wish I hadn't just lived through this devastating lesson! I wish my family hadn't. I wish my neighbors hadn't.

And that's the gut-level urgency with which I now share the rest of this book with you.

My analysis shows a far more widespread disaster on the horizon. For far too many, it may be as serious as a house fire. The retirement crisis surely will threaten and shorten lives.

But I'm hopeful—always hopeful—because I have renewed faith in what I have experienced throughout my life. I know that we can join together and survive this great retirement cliff ahead of us, over which millions are likely to fall into poverty.

I cannot thank you enough for picking up my book. Together, we can work to provide a better future for us all.

2

Introducing "The Future Poor"

Given my surname, let's start with the Grimm news: Our current approach to retirement is going to leave a vast number of middle-class Americans in dire need in their senior years—a looming crisis I call "the future poor." That's where millions of us will be living if we don't collectively rethink our current assumptions about retirement.

But, if we understand the looming crisis—as you will, if you continue reading this book—then there's good news, too: There are things we can do to prevent this social catastrophe.

Let's start with: How did we get here? The current experiment with retirement emerged after World War II and became the standard. You worked until you were 65 and then you were entitled to leave the workforce. In theory, and in most cases, you had the resources and support needed to do this. Pretty soon the experiment became the cultural expectation most of us share as Americans. Now, generations have grown up with faith that this system would keep working as it did for decades. If you are like me, you grew up with this expectation: Go to school, get a good job, save for retirement, and then enjoy the golden sunset with all your basic needs met.

But trouble is rolling in, especially for the vast majority of us under the age of 50. The financial situation has changed and it isn't what we thought. We're not living in the 1950s anymore, of course, but the roaring '60s and '70s are gone, as well—and even the booming 1980s seem like an entirely different world. Life before the iPhone's debut in 2007 is a forgotten time. Now it is the 2020s and the fact is that many people are woefully behind in their retirement planning. Savings are low, home ownership is low, expenses are high, and so on. Some already are realizing that the nostalgic dream of "retirement" is not in the cards. Others are still living with that dream without realizing that ideal is far from reality.

Fortunately for you, this particular Grimm believes in happy endings—and from many years as a financial advisor helping individuals and companies cope with today's economic reality, I can tell you: This book is not a fairy tale.

In fact, the warning that runs throughout this book is that our current experiment with retirement must come to an end. It is not going to work for the future. Even looking back, we can see that it has not been good for people to have adopted the entitled view of retirement that sprang up in the years after World War II—the idea that retiring at 65 is a fundamental American right.

That sense of entitlement is a relatively new phenomenon within human history. Unfortunately, we do not have a viable replacement. What we have is a "perfect storm" of worldview, economic factors, and social structures that equates to an impoverished future. We have built a system that is leaving millions of Americans dependent upon themselves to fund 20–30 years of income after they stop working. Furthermore, conventional financial advice will not get us off the road to becoming the future poor. We need something new. Death is coming for this version of retirement one way or another. My hope is that it is because we have given birth to something better. Together we need to pivot and create more just and viable structures, practices and values that enable financial well-being for all people throughout life—before it's too late.

This book is a hopeful vision of the future that does require a significant set of shifts that we must undertake together. Our national trends are clear that, if we do not make these shifts, economic troubles await us in a few decades to the degree that there will be no option for any type of retirement for most of us. My hope is that we do not wait until then to wake up and realize we had a problem all along.

In the book *Who Not How*, Dr. Benjamin Hardy outlines the philosophy of Dan Sullivan, one of the foremost coaches for entrepreneurs. In this process, one of the keys to finding people to join you in any project or venture is to create a one-pager called an "impact filter" that simply answers a couple key questions.

So, here is my—

Impact filter for *The Future Poor* project:

Here is what success looks like:

Success reshapes the current expectation of entitled retirement to something more conducive to human flourishing—socially, psychologically, and economically. Success includes rebuilding the key socioeconomic factors a society requires for the welfare and well-being of its people throughout their lives. Yes, that is a vast undertaking involving all aspects of family, community, social, economic, and political life. But the good news is: Our nation did it before—and we can do it again. We must return to traditional values that today are widely defined as the social determinants of health by public health experts around the world, including strengthening our collective economic stability, healthcare systems, and our social and community relationships. As the ethical responsibility to one another grows, my hope is that we can work together to solve the major systemic issues we need to rebuild. On a practical level for individuals and families, we need to reshape our assumptions about financial planning to better serve people in this ever more challenging world of the 2020s and beyond.

Here is why this project is so important:

If we don't take steps now, the vast majority of our population is moving toward poverty—we will become the future poor. In the United States, we have created a situation where we are making it untenable for those under the age of 50 (sub-50) and those making under $150,000 of income annually (sub-150) to have the resources needed to provide for their needs in their post-productive years.

Here is what we stand to gain if we succeed:

We stand to gain personal financial flourishing that expands and creates financial well-being for our family, friends, colleagues, and our broader community. This is not some "pie in the sky" vision. In the past, Americans have come together and reshaped our collective future, despite fewer resources, limited knowledge, archaic technology, and reduced social awareness. The power of capital and money have become something greater than they ought to be, but that does not mean we ought to eliminate these resources. Quite the opposite. Capital usage for society's well-being is central and that is where success actually rests, not in any day's stock price, profit margin, or simply the amount of cash in our pockets. What awaits us in our success is a new kind of financial flourishing that we have yet to know.

Here is what is at stake if we fail:

What is at stake if we fail is the ushering of more and more people into a lower and lower socioeconomic situation as they age. This is not something to take lightly, as it may be the undoing of all that our financial strength is based upon. If we fail, we all suffer a financial downturn. Our entire economic system depends on our ongoing ability to keep purchasing. Without that, companies lose their value and assets collapse. Older individuals that must work into older age clog the workforce, keeping younger generations from work—this is a repetition of a pattern we saw 150 years ago and it is not good.

I want us to solve future poverty.

I want you to join me in this.

I hope you will join me for the sake of those who may be in the greatest danger of poverty.

I also want you to join me for your own sake, as well.

So, here we go.

3

The Origin Story

There is a 99% chance that if you are reading this, you are not in the top 1% of wealth earners in America. That's OK! This book is for us. Until we turn a DeLorean into an actual time machine, 100% of us are on the road to the future—the destination of being older, hopefully wiser, and for most, some version of retiring from work and shifting to other interests that matter far more.

What about you? What comes to mind when you think of the future?

Do you envision a future like in *The Matrix* where we are at war with machines? Perhaps you think we are all living in a simulation now.

Is what you see a plot like the movie *Terminator*? That was one of my grandfather's favorite films. Perhaps today that looks like Skynet and AI taking over, causing all types of problems. We are only a few years away from 2029, the year it all goes down in that movie.

Maybe your imagined future is more like *Back to the Future II* where in 2015 we were supposed to have flying cars, self-lacing Nike's, and hoverboards. We sure missed that target, even though we do have a bunch of people trying to go to space, so that counts for something!

What about your future, specifically? What sort of future do you see for yourself when you are 60, 70, and then 80 years old? Maybe you have never thought about it because it is a long way off and there is plenty to think of right now. Perhaps, you are already there, or very close, so you have a better picture.

More than likely, your vision of the future is something like your current life with family, friends, and a career—only improved.

Within your vision of the future, what do you desire?

What goals or achievements are you currently working toward?

What things would you wish to do—or own?

Are there relationships or experiences you wish to have?

What about financially? Where do you see yourself in terms of your future income?

In my years of advising clients, I have found: 100% of them see a better financial future than the one they currently have. Yes, *everyone* hopes to be doing better in the future! I have never met with a business owner who says, "I'd really like our revenue to decline next year and our expenses rise." Or, "Our goal for the next quarter is to have our stock price drop." I have never worked for a company where the stated goal was less sales growth and worse profits. Likewise, I have never met with an individual or couple for financial planning who says they would like to be worse off than they currently are. No one has asked me to help them save less, acquire more debt or have less money in their bank account. No one ever asks: "Can you help my portfolio to drop 25%?"

This may seem obvious to you. The hope of growth and progress is not only an essential part of being human—it's the framework on which the Western world was built. We can easily intuit what having more money means for our situation. More importantly, we know and fear what having less money means.

Most people I advise do not have ambitions to end up with Jeff Bezos or Elon Musk money—they just want to know they are doing the right things with what they have. They do not want to be poor.

Fair enough, but why don't we want to be poor?

Being poor is a dread of its own, an umbrella fear that influences the quality of every aspect of life. A quick glance at Maslow's famous hierarchy of needs paints the picture: Food, shelter, security, and health all sit at the foundational level of our needs. Losing those resources is a terrifying situation for individuals and families alike.

Let me ask you a question in order to bring this back to you and me and our road to the future: Do you want to be poor in the future?

I am guessing you answered with an emphatic: "NO!"

Me too! No part of me wants that as my future. But, if we were having this conversation over a cup of coffee, I would say honestly:

"You are going to be living at or below the U.S. poverty level when you retire."

Take a minute to think about that sentence. Then, read it again from the first-person perspective:

"I am going to be living at or below the U.S. poverty level when I retire."

And, yes, I know! You likely have a reason this does not apply to you. Do any of your reasons include the following?

"I have a good job."

"I make decent money."

"I contribute to my 401(k) and get a match."

"I have money in savings."

"I have a Roth IRA."

"I own a home (or recently bought one)."

"I will get an inheritance."

"I am not poor."

Those may be true and potential steps in the right direction but should be no comfort when it comes to what I will repeat:

"You are going to be living at or below the U.S. poverty level when you retire."

If you still do not believe me, keep on reading just to make sure! I do hope this is not the case for you and many more of us. I also believe it is better to confront this possibility now rather than find out the hard way, like most retirees. My encouragement is to continue reading so you can begin to see how this is the largest hidden ethical crisis facing us today.

We are rapidly approaching a world where we are the future poor. This particular social and ethical crisis requires many people and perspectives to be part of a solution. This problem also surfaces individual and collective issues that will require individual and collective work to put us on a road to a better destination than the one we are currently following in the U.S.

'Please, tell me there's hope!'

In discussing the premise of this book with friends, they respond: "Please, tell me there's hope!"

In her 2023 book, *A Healthy State of Panic*, Farnoosh Torabi, a best-selling financial author and former CNBC host, speaks to similar sentiments. She writes, "They want assurance ... will this work out?"

Why?

"Because money moves are life moves and the stakes are high," Torabi writes. She urges her readers to uncover and face financial fears. Like Torabi, I wish to do two things moving forward. First, she says that her book is "your permission to feel unapologetically scared." I began this book with "Grimm news" in the first sentence. You have permission to be concerned. I am. My friends are—especially after hearing me discuss what follows in this book with them—but that is not all there is. We must also take the second step of moving forward, past the fear, and ending with action and hope.

So, back to my friends and their plea, and maybe yours!

I quickly assure them, and you, that there is hope, but like all matters of great consequence, it is complex. Still, a lot can be done between now and when we all arrive at retirement. Think of the subsequent chapters in this book as a journey through these challenges in the hope that understanding the issues and how we got here will help us to engineer a solution. What you will find moving forward is a book born from observation. My financial analysis is solid and detailed enough to satisfy most professionals—and it is accessible so that hopefully all readers will be able to apply its information immediately. I wrote this book to engage everyone to reconsider the road we are on—and to decide for yourself whether that road will work for you, your family, your friends, and society.

This book is not my strategy for you to get rich, achieve peace with your money, or tell you which products, investments, or strategies are better than others. While there is merit in many of the strategies that financial advisors and money gurus like to follow, my intent is to go beyond these. We are looking at something much broader than your individual finances or which investments to pick. I am licensed to assist with those financial matters, but that is not the aim in this journey we are undertaking to ensure a better future. My goal is to move you and the rest of our country forward on a road that leads us to a better destination.

In my work and life, I rely on the principle of *credibility*—the idea that people trust certain other people because they know they will do the job the right way. When people come to me hoping for advice that will earn them a promotion to assistant manager, store manager, or beyond, I always say: "Your coworkers will decide." Credibility is the currency of successful work-places, marketplaces, and relationships. Successful employees know the value of credibility and model this value. In years of analyzing organizations and businesses to advise them on better practices, I start by asking: "Who do people go to?" Answers to that question quickly point me toward the real sources of credibility. These are people others seek out in times of need, who serve and step in when needed; they're ultimately the people others trust and follow. In all my years of consulting, I've never promoted anyone—they did that themselves by demonstrating credibility.

So, what makes me uniquely credible to write this book? To answer that I'll give you a brief resumé. Let's start with my bachelor's degree in ethics and a minor in psychology along with a master's degree in theological studies.

I have been captivated by the history of the 20th century from an early age and that interest only deepened when my college ethics professor said we should develop a worldview or belief system that can make sense of the Holocaust. That perspective challenges me to this day to be practical in my work, so that it makes sense for today and the potential of future catastrophes.

While in graduate school, I began working in hospitality management at a large brand-new Marriott convention hotel. That began my business management training. Over the next two decades, I worked in food and beverage operations in international airports, led multimillion-dollar operations in national brands, ran operations for a cupcake company, and did several years in the nonprofit sector, taking leadership over finance, HR, ops, IT, and almost every other department at some point. Beyond handling the business management aspects of multimillion-dollar operations, I had the privilege of working with thousands of people from every type of background. This has shaped my concern for a wide variety of people—a concern for our larger community that I hope you share.

Professionally, I am a licensed financial advisor and stockbroker with all of the federal and state licenses that accompany those titles. I will not speak much about my financial practice in this book, as that is not this book's purpose. As a financial advisor, I have studied and been certified on retirement strategies since that is a central component of most financial planning. All of these experiences contribute to my developing a financial advising model that accounts for what you are about to read in The Future Poor.

I am a *synthesizer* in the areas of philosophy, history, finance, and ethics—and that is what leads me to share this unique perspective on money, ethics, and the direction of our country.

This book began during the COVID pandemic, as we all had more time than ever to be home. This time period also shed a lot of light on the financial situations of a majority of Americans. Many couldn't work because their workplaces were closed. Businesses shut down. Stimulus checks and PPP loans tried to keep everyone afloat. Alarmingly low savings and serious housing issues illuminated some of the broader systemic issues within the American economy.

Simultaneously, during the end of 2019 and early 2020, I was doing in-depth study of how income works in retirement as I was doing more of that type of planning for my clients. Reading the latest research was certainly alarming—but it was applying those findings to my study of retirement when I began to get truly worried. Difficult economic and financial situations seldom create a good future for individuals without something drastic occurring. Thus, I began looking at the road we are on from the perspective of financial ethics and began to see what very well may be the greatest ethical oversight of this generation.

Where money and ethics tend to converge presently is in looking at the state of those currently experiencing poverty and developing public policies focused on these situations. While it is important to give attention and resources to these present concerns, it is also equally important to give attention to the trajectory of large segments of our population. This is where I am focused: The scope of financial ethics needs to include those who are the future poor.

Let's do the numbers—they're compelling!

To be honest, my motivation to attend to this question began from a selfish place. I wanted to know what I would need to have in an account to provide an income above poverty level. I hope this is now a question you are considering!

To begin the exploration, I sought out what the U.S. poverty level is today for a couple since I am married and plan to stay that way.

Any guesses on what that amount might be?

My guess is that number you thought of is far below what you are currently earning. Using the math of the *safe withdrawal rate*, all you need to do is multiply that by 25 and you get the amount you need in the retirement account. (Safe withdrawal rate is an important concept that will help you and continue to be a crucial part of understanding the situation we face.)

Back when I started, here was the math: $ 17,240 \times 25 = \$431,000$ (future income desired x 25 = the bag of money you need.)

In 2024, it's even worse! It is $511,000.

This means that the account you pull from today needs $511,000 in it, if you desire a poverty-level retirement of $20,440 a year. Now, $511,000 hardly sounds like poverty and in many ways it isn't. However, in terms of being able to have an income for 20 or 30 years, it most certainly is!

Those numbers terrify me!

Thanks to our access to U.S. Census data, published research, and the magic of Google, it doesn't take much investigation to get a handle on the current state of things. The Federal Reserve reports that 28% of nonretirees have no forms of retirement savings. The Fed also reports that women, Black and Hispanic people, and the segment of our population with lower levels of education trail behind their counterparts. The 2021 Survey of Income and Program Participation (SIPP) by the Census Bureau revealed that the median value of retirement accounts was $30,000 and revealed the same inequity factors as the Fed. The Government Accountability Office report on households aged 51–64 revealed that only those in the highest 20% had over $100,000 saved for retirement.

Reputable finance journals, like *Forbes* or *The Wall Street Journal*, report similar findings about how low retirement savings are and how we need to save more. Financial firms publish similar reports. Vanguard, one of the largest and most popular investment advisory firms, publishes an annual report called "How America Saves." They report that the median account balance was $27,376 in 2022 and that account balances were down an average of 15% from the previous year.

Where do you see yourself in these dire reports? Maybe you see the problem that I see: *We do not have a good enough jump-start on retirement to even come close to making it over the next 20–30 years.*

My analysis is that 95% of us are continuing down the same road toward our later years in life—unaware of where we all are heading. Many are past the point of no return and are perhaps realizing their destination is living at or below the U.S. poverty level in retirement.

In summary, the middle class in America has the worst time value of money (TVM) financial equation we have seen in post-WWII American history. TVM is a mathematical calculation that those of us in the financial world use to calculate the future value of an investment based on the current amount saved, a hypothetical rate of return and how long the investment is allowed to grow. With it, we can project a future value of the accounts people have, like 401(k)s or IRAs.

We do not have enough savings to start with.

We do not have enough savings each month.

We do not have enough time to correct it.

I'm scared. Perhaps you are scared, as well.

The point of this new awareness is take action—and that's why I devoted the last four years to exploring these challenges.

I now believe there are ways we can respond together—before it is too late.

4

Who Are the Future Poor?

They're us.

That's the short answer for most people reading this book—if we don't work together and take steps, that is.

To better define those at risk of becoming the future poor, let's start with a more familiar phrase: "the middle class." This group's classic features are jobs, home ownership, a family, probably a college education, and some other qualities of the stereotypical American Dream—like a plan for retirement. But what is required for retirement? We can calculate that from current savings, income earning, savings ability, and time before reaching age 65. And when we make that calculation, we realize the future poor is a group I describe as sub-50/sub-150—meaning people ages 50 and under who are making less than $150,000 a year. Around 95% of people in America fit into one or both of these categories.

I wrote this book because that enormous sub-50/sub-150 group by and large doesn't see a problem—and that is not good for encouraging change. The sub-50 group thinks there is time. The sub-150, especially the more you approach and pass the $100,000 mark in annual income, thinks they are making enough money. Time and money can be very deceptive when dealing with financial matters. I want you to take the situation seriously and make your starting place one of being included in the at-risk category rather than thinking you are not.

For the purposes of clarity, I'm using "the middle class" to describe people whose income is between $50,000 and $150,000. When you see sub-150, you can know that I am referring to everyone that makes less than $150,000. This distinction will be clearer as we dive deeper into the moral situation and the need for additional concern for those who are in even lower income-earning brackets.

The heart of the problem

If you go to Amazon and search books on retirement you will get everything from "strategies to grow wealth," to "transitioning to retirement," to "retirement-planning workbooks," to "retiring early," to "fun things to do in retirement," and so on. Some even focus on FIRE—the Financially Independent, Retire Early movement. As a financial advisor, I have devoted a lot of time to studying strategy and helping clients with their retirement plans. So, I have read many of these books and love some of them.

However, most of these books follow a similar trajectory. They reel you in thinking about your dream vision of retirement, freedom, and adventure. Isn't that the great alternative to long work weeks and grinding away for most of your adulthood? The first 25% of many books give some suggestions for thinking about income and the size that your nest egg should be. They focus you on your dreams and what vision you have for your newfound time and financial freedom. Then, they spend the remainder of the book pulling the rug out from underneath you with a good dose of retirement reality and how you should probably have a realistic plan versus the dreamy one you may be developing. These books can be helpful, but they do not involve the detailed financial planning that it takes to understand retirement and get it right.

It is important to know that traditional financial planning considers a couple key terms. Broadly, the two main ones are "accumulation" and then "distribution." Accumulation is the challenging phase of collecting and growing money, while distribution is the fun phase of spending what you've collected. Within these two phases are all kinds of accumulation and distribution vehicles, philosophies, approaches, methods, gurus, and the like. Accumulation typically involves funding your 401(k), buying a house, saving money, and investing money. Distribution is the simpler idea of how to turn what you have accumulated into income or a "paycheck" to live on. I wish there was a one-size-fits-all way to guarantee success. I would do it myself and it would make my profession as an advisor a lot easier.

The truth is that there is no single method or philosophy that can guarantee success and this book will not advocate for one. Among all the people who have followed step-by-step plans in a box, there are success stories and failures. People accumulate money successfully and unsuccessfully using every strategy available. For every strategy that is criticized, there are countless examples of success. I am bringing this up because often we fall into the trap of believing we did not follow the "right" plan and so we are in this position. While that can be a contributing factor, and we will look at that, behind the scenes the issue is not with any of the strategies that gurus and advisors recommend.

There is no universal plan, despite what you may read or hear:

- Real estate versus investing in the stock market is not the source of this crisis.
- Whether or not we have 3-6 months in an "emergency fund" is not the source.
- Maxing out your retirement accounts or using cash for everything are not sure-fire solutions to this crisis.
- Even debt is not the entire issue.

No, the critical issue arises from not understanding how much income we can expect in the distribution phase of our life given how much accumulation we have been able to accomplish. The sub-50/sub-150 population is way behind both financially—and in their understanding of this future reality.

For example, most of us naturally focus on accumulation as a financial solution. However, over time, I have become convinced that distribution is more important to plan for than accumulation.

Can you answer these questions:

- Where is your retirement income going to come from?
- How much is it going to be every year for the rest of your life?
- And then, what are all the expenses you are going to need to cover in your retirement years?

In years of meeting with clients, I have yet to find anyone who knows those answers to a certainty. Most don't even have an estimate. Even my older clients who are in their 60s and getting ready for retirement don't know. That's why they are terrified when they seek out advice from me and others.

In answering the first question, the most common response is a hesitant: "Social Security?"

"Ok!" I say, "Have you looked to see your estimated income?"

Inevitably the answer is no—or they mention receiving a statement every once in a while, which a lot of people throw away.

So, here's your first action item: Go to the Social Security Administration website, www.ssa.gov, and create an account right now. They will provide you an estimate, with the disclaimer that it has the potential to be less. You can see how much of your current income your estimate covers. This is an important step in understanding the future reality. Keep in mind two things that most people don't realize about Social Security. Up to 85% of your benefit may be subject to income tax—and part of your benefit may need to be used to purchase the different parts of Medicare. Both reduce your take-home benefit.

The second response about retirement income is, "I have a 401(k)." This is probably the retirement account we are most familiar with, and some are useful. However, the 401(k) reply is tied to an underlying assumption that confuses a retirement *account* with a retirement *plan*. The myth of having a 401(k) is that you have retirement covered because of a belief that contributing 5% and getting a match from your employer is an effective retirement solution. The 401(k) takes the planning and guesswork out of retirement for most people. But most people have no idea what the potential account value will be in the future or how this translates to retirement income.

A third, and increasingly common answer is, "I hope to get an inheritance."

Yes, some people are blessed with an inheritance. An influx of cash into any system tends to provide relief, increased stability, and openness to more opportunity. You see it with businesses and individual finances alike. However, there is a dark side to this. In a later chapter I will discuss the pitfalls of inheritance money.

All in all, no one quite knows whether they will have enough money for retirement. Those who are more hopeful have a vague sense that they will be making about what they do now. Others think they will figure it out in time because they are young. The small remainder of people are a bit terrified by the unknowns looming in their future—and want to begin working on this challenge.

If you see yourself reflected in one of those responses that I have just described—I hope you realize that none of these scenarios will guarantee success. These questions are alarming! And, yes, I am intentionally ringing that alarm bell because the reality is that in retirement the majority of us will have inadequate levels of monthly income.

Understanding the distribution phase

The theory and mechanics of the distribution phase center on a fear and a rule.

First, the fear: The number one fear of retirees is that they will outlive the money that they have accumulated. Most retirees are not frivolous or lavish in their retirement years. Far from it! Most retires adapt to cutbacks—rather than the leisure, travel, and freedom shown in retirement advertisements. Fear of running out of money is very real, especially with ever-increasing life expectancy. That longevity brings some of the most expensive phases in retirement: medical expenses and end-of-life care, not to mention burial expenses. The equation of living longer plus increasing medical expenses (often not covered by government plans) equals the need for more and more money.

But how can you know if you will run out of money?

The initial answer came in the form of an extensive study that was done by financial advisor William Bengen in the 1990s to determine something known as "safe withdrawal rate." The study concluded with what has famously become the 4% rule. In most cases, you can safely take 4% out of your accounts each year and the money will not run out over 30 years. While not a fixed rule, the math works out because it falls in the middle of the range of 3-6% annual increases in interest rates and market returns. The bottom line is: You are not able to withdraw significant portions from your bag of retirement savings if you want your money to last.

For example, let's say you have $500,000 in your retirement accounts. The 4% rule says that you can safely withdraw $20,000 each year and never run out of money. Given the actual state of the economy at the time you are withdrawing, that number could be anywhere from $15,000-$30,000 a year. In a year the market is down, it may be wisest to withdraw $0. That range is still well below the median income in the U.S. and is probably far less than most of us are comfortable with receiving each year.

It is this combination of fear and the 4% rule that first caused me concern as a young advisor. The thesis of this book was born from a question after studying the safe withdrawal rate and the financial philosophies surrounding it. That simple question was, "What do you need in a retirement account today to withdraw 4% and be at the U.S. poverty level of income for a couple?"

The problem is that our brain monetizes stuff very well, but only in immediate terms. We can look at a lump sum of money and immediately we know what we can buy with it and what we would want to buy with it. If I say to you, "You will have $750,000 in your account when you retire," you are likely to get excited because that is a lot of money! You can immediately translate that into a house, car, trips, and other things you want. But this leaves out the most important purchase of our future, our future income, and this is one of the major ways we are on the road to being the future poor.

Why do we forget this? We have not had to think of our income from the perspective of purchasing future income. Millions of Americans have not had to think about life after our weekly or monthly paycheck ends. We work; we get paid. We do not "buy" income—we use our income to buy. In retirement, the game changes. We no longer offer our effort and service in exchange for a paycheck. Instead, we exchange the amount we have accumulated for a "paycheck" that we hope lasts as long as we do. This is the piece that has been left out of financial planning for far too long and why we must focus on the distribution phase more than we have.

This idea of your future income—or what I call your "next paycheck"—is not a new idea. Things like income annuities, where you give your money to a money manager in exchange for a guaranteed income for the rest of your life, have their origins back in ancient Rome. Annuities were born of an ancient human problem that required a viable solution for the money manager and the person needing income in their post-working or post-producing years. Somehow, though, this idea of our next paycheck has more recently escaped our attention.

Where does "income" come from when you do not have a job? If you have ever been without work for a period of time you have certainly had to deal with that question. In some cases, it comes from savings, investments, or other sources like businesses or rental properties. There may be some government support for a time. Post-retirement it comes from you and you alone—with a bit of help from the government. And the real kicker is that you may have to generate 20 to 30 years of income on your own.

Here's your second action item: Ask yourself, "How much does it cost to buy 20–30 years of income?"

Some financial industry professionals do not believe this situation to be as bad as I think it is. They offer a wide range of distribution models. For example, they may shrink the number of years you need to fund—or they may advise shrinking the amount of money you expect to leave behind.

Let's say you have accumulated $750,000 to use for your retirement. The 4% rule says you can take out $30,000 a year and never run out of money. Essentially, you would leave $750,000 behind as inheritance. Let's say you want to spend it all in 10 years' time and do a lot before old age sets in. If so, over a 10-year period, you could probably take out $75,000–$100,000 a year, depending on how the chunk of money is invested. After 10 years, you may be down to $0 and living off Social Security or other means. Perhaps you want to spend it all in a matter of 5 years. You could probably use $150,000-200,000 a year and have a pretty fun 5 years! After those fun 5 years, though, I'm not sure what would happen to you.

Of course, this isn't the only "rule." Most financial pros follow a methodology that works things out step by step or in some order of operations. Some say you should save eight times your last year's income for a proper nest egg. Or perhaps you have heard that you will need only 80% of your current income in retirement. There are other targets that have been set, usually involving some multiple at various ages. You might have heard that, by 30, you should have the equivalent of one year's salary saved, then by 40, 3 times, and 6 times by 50—and so on.

Here's another popular model: For saving, step one is to have 3–6 months of emergency funds in cash. Step two is to contribute up to the match of your 401(k). Three, max out a Roth IRA. Four, max out your 401(k), and so on.

At the heart of most popular finance books is a formula like these—methods for accumulating with the idea that you will be taken care of in the future, sometimes with the assumption that you will need less income in the future.

Questioning the conventional wisdom

I am skeptical.

Why?

Because we are planning for tomorrow with yesterday's information. We have no idea what the future holds. There may be changes to the economy— or some other major social determinant like public health or climate or the cost of accessing commodities like water or fuel—that we cannot foresee. If you are optimistic, you might assume that future improvements in Social Security—or other public programs—are going to account for such major changes. We cannot rely on outdated advice or advice that was created for a different time for today's situation and certainly not the future state.

But we still are left with the reality that the majority of the sub-50/sub-150 people have not accumulated nearly enough for even a basic retirement. The issue is one of mathematics, the reality of what income will be for people, and the ramifications of those numbers. Let's look at a few cases. Hopefully, one of these will mirror your current situation or at least be close.

We will look at three 40-year-old individuals and we will use a time value of money (TVM) calculator to do the math. If you are unfamiliar with TVM calculators, I recommend Googling the term or checking out a YouTube video or two. Time value of money is how we can calculate the growth of money based on how much we start with, how many years we are letting it grow, how much we are regularly adding, and by what interest rate it is growing. I use my TVM calculator multiple times a day. Aside from being my favorite app on my phone, it is the great reality check of money math.

Patty

$100,000 saved in their retirement accounts.

They make $75,000 a year at their jobs.

They contribute 5% and get a 5% match in their retirement accounts.

TVM calculation

Present value: $100,000

Annual retirement savings: $7,500

Rate of return: 6%

(I am comfortable with 6% for long-term calculations to account for market changes and the effect that several market corrections can have on your account growth.)

Period: 25 years (to get them to age 65)

Drumroll ... Future value of their account: $840,670

Retirement income using 4%: $33,600

To get to their current income they need: $1,875,000

They would need to be saving: $26,352/year (almost $20,000 more than they currently are)

Jack

$50,000 saved in their retirement accounts.

They make $60,000 a year at their jobs.

They contribute 5% and get a 5% match in their retirement accounts.

TVM calculation

Present value: $50,000

Annual retirement savings: $6,000

Rate of return: 6%

Period: 25 years

Drumroll ... Future value of their account: $543,780

Retirement income using 4%: $21,751

To get to their current income they need: $1,500,000

They would need to be saving: $23,428/year (they need 4x the savings)

Sam

$50,000 saved in their retirement accounts.

They make $100,000 a year at their jobs.

They contribute 5% and get a 5% match in their retirement accounts.

TVM calculation

Present value: $50,000

Annual retirement savings: $10,000

Rate of return: 6%

Period: 25 years

Drumroll ... Future value of their account: $763,238

Retirement income using 4%: $30,529

To get to their current income they need: $2,500,000

They would need to be saving: $41,655/year (over 40% of their income)

Each of these examples illustrates the gap at the center of my thesis making up *The Future Poor* and the reality of future income being low. Sure, another advisor may show you 8% returns or more, often touted as an average market return or a better investment. That hypothetical number will be mathematically greater. But Sam is still behind by almost $1.5 million with an 8% return, so what do we do?

That gap is in several forms. The first is in understanding how much retirement income you can reasonably expect from your accumulated savings. In each example, the income is about one-third of their current annual earnings. People's expenses are reduced in most cases in retirement—but not by that level. The second gap is a comparison between what they are saving versus what they would need to save to have a similar level of income. The third gap is in trusting that the stock market alone will support their future, because that can be problematic.

The nail in the coffin

There may be some ways that the scenarios above work out favorably over the next 25–30 years. In each of them, there is a resource pool of $500,000–$1 million. That is certainly an enormous resource for the future. In the situation of a sustained income for retirement, it may fall short. But that is just the beginning of truly thinking about the future poor and future income.

Like many of the great game shows on TV, the host reveals what you are playing for and says those glorious words, "But wait ... there's more!" I told you at the beginning that this was a book that took after my last name of Grimm, and this is one of those moments. This one isn't an additional prize. This is the case of discovering that what's behind door No. 2 is something you don't want!

This is because there is one variable out there that is seldom discussed related to retirement savings and future income. This variable is the nail in the coffin for understanding the future state of the sub-50/sub-150. That variable is *the effect of inflation on those future dollars*. We all know it's there and feel it in different ways, but because of its gradual nature we are mostly used to it. Yet, when we look back in time, we can see it pretty clearly. When I started driving in the 90s, $1 could get me one gallon of gas. Today, that same $1 gets me ¼ of a gallon of gas. I live in California, so it's even worse!

So why is this so critical in thinking about the future poor? It rests in the fact that about every 20–30 years, depending on what's happening out there in the economy, your $1 loses 50% or more of its buying power. Like the example with gas, it now takes 4–5 times the number of dollars to get the same gallon of gasoline. The same is true when we look at projecting a future income. We must think of it in terms of future dollars and future buying power, not today's dollars and today's buying power.

A simple general rule I follow is to reduce that future income total by 50% when thinking 20 or more years out. Using Sam from above, a $2.5 million dollar account will be worth the same as a $1.25 million account is today. Also, $100,000 of income today is worth $50,000 in the future. Most retirement accounts have some sort of projection of a future income based on what you are saving. They will say "this account's going to get you $4,000/month when you retire." That sounds great, but in future dollars, that is potentially only worth $2,000/month.

I find that about this time in the discussion, a few things start to happen. First, it is very hard to project out and think of the "future you." Especially 30 years out. It's as if that is a completely different person who may or may not exist. This is a normal phenomenon and was studied by Hal Hershfield, a professor at UCLA and author of the book *Your Future Self*. Hershfield's study reveals that planning for "future you" is like planning for a stranger. The problem with this kind of projection is compounded by our societal focus on "The Now" and our tendency to push long-term things far off into the future.

With retirement being so far out from today, there is an impulse in us to think about it later since there is still time. Let's consider Sam from above trying to save over $40K a year. If Sam waits 5 years, they now must save $60K a year for 20 years to hit the same goal. That's an additional $200K just to get to the same spot. Yikes!

At this point, you may be crying out: *Too much math!*

That is something I am quite familiar with and normally leave a lot of the complicated calculations out of many financial conversations. Yet, it is important to do the math here, to move it from being simply my theory to a reality we all must face.

Keep with me, please. I know this can be daunting. In fact, when friends have asked me what I'm writing, I have been telling them: "I'm writing an uplifting book about how we are all going to be poor in the future."

And the overall message of this book is uplifting. Keep reading. We'll hit the inspiring parts as we come to terms with these challenges we face.

5

What is "Retirement"?

For millennia, there was no widespread expectation of retirement because of another grim reality: People died young. Life expectancy was so short that most people were gone decades before what we now consider to be retirement age. Most of those who did survive into their 70s, 80s, and 90s lived with their multigenerational families and contributed to daily life as they were able. Most cultures around the world were agrarian and those fortunate enough to have family homes expected to live there all their lives surrounded by younger generations.

Of course, there are examples of retirement planning that date back to the Roman Empire. The Roman army provided something like a pension for those who survived the grueling challenges of military life. In the urban areas that sprang up around the empire, annuities were offered by bankers who would exchange your money for a monthly guaranteed return.

The Bible records a parable of Jesus about the noteworthy nature of investing. In Matthew 25:14, Jesus speaks of a master giving bags of money to three servants. The first received five bags of silver, invested it and got five more. The second received two bags of silver and did the same. He invested and got two more. The third took his one bag of silver and dug a hole, threw it in, and buried it to keep it safe. The master returns and praises the two who invested and earned more. The third who did nothing was scolded for doing nothing. Jesus goes on to say that the master suggests that the lazy servant could have at least deposited his silver in the bank and earned interest.

The origin of what we now call "retirement" was a major change in the course of human history that sprang up only a little more than a century ago. Until 1900, average life expectancy, even in Europe and the U.S., was still in the low 40s! Most people living in Europe and the U.S. simply hoped to keep living and working a few years longer to help raise their children. They weren't worrying about accumulating enough wealth to live independently for many decades.

Highlights of retirement history

Most Americans aren't aware that our expectations of retirement owe a debt to German history in particular, because Chancellor Otto von Bismarck instituted what became a global model for old-age insurance in 1889. Historians debate Bismarck's motives to this day, but one of his goals was to incentivize older workers to exit the workforce. German industrialization had become so successful that workers were holding onto their jobs as long as possible. Young people entering their working years could not find jobs and that was creating an economic challenge. Part of the solution proposed by Bismarck was to provide a basic income for older workers and make it feasible for them to step away from work and still be able to make it financially. Initially, Germany set the retirement age at 70, then nearly three decades later that age was lowered to 65.

During our own Great Depression, older Americans found the economic devastation particularly challenging since work was sparse and they had no money. The New Deal under President Roosevelt worked to create jobs, jump-start the economy, and provide for the needs of those who had no other means. By the time our Social Security Act passed in 1935, the German idea had been catching on around the world—including across the United States. Regional and industry-specific plans already were popping up. Thirty states came up with their own systems. Railroad workers were protected by a national system by 1934. To organize the tidal wave that was building nationwide, President Roosevelt pushed through a whole series of new programs all wrapped up in that one Social Security Act, including Unemployment Insurance, Aid to Dependent Children, Old Age Insurance, and Old Age Assistance. By 1937, 20 million Social Security cards had been issued!

Still, even with all that background—the world had seen nothing quite resembling what emerged in the post-World War II era in America. At the time, America was getting back on its feet in a new and radical way.

Retirement history at a glance

There are many other in-depth books about our changing cultural expectations of aging—and the financial history of family welfare. But, because this book is about our looming crisis in retirement, we need to understand the basics of this history.

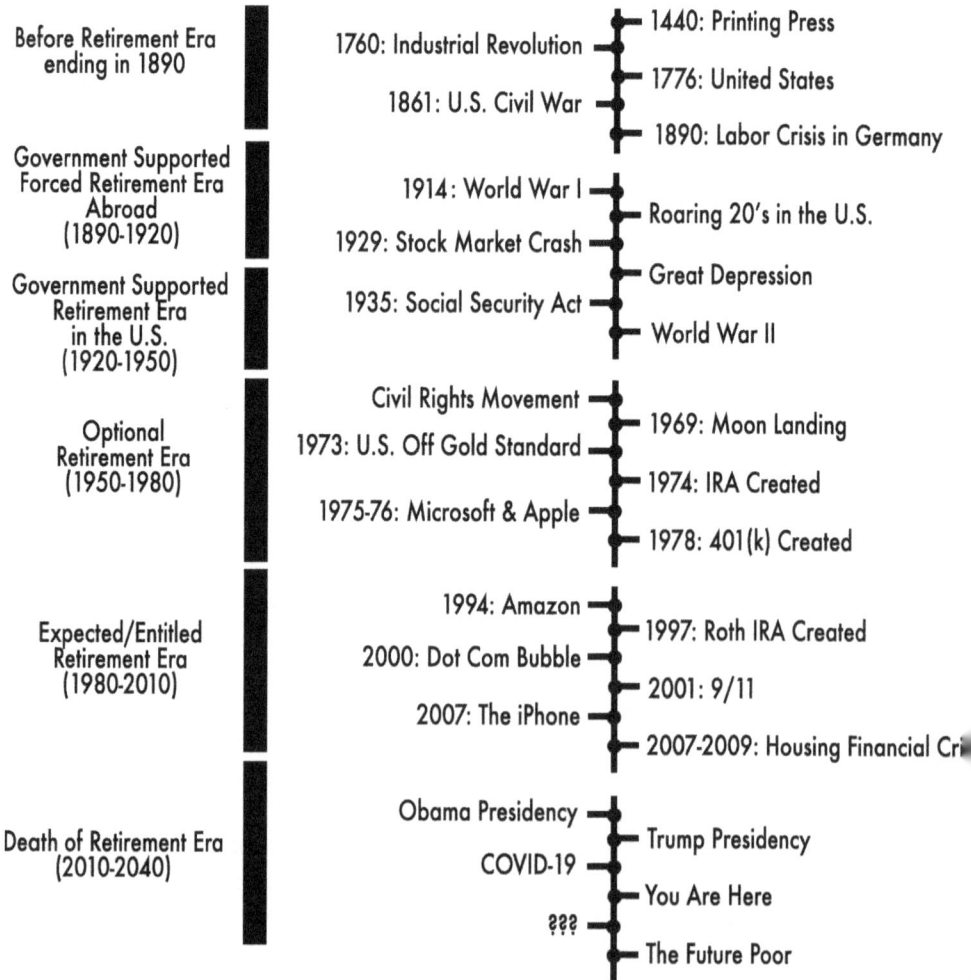

Era	Left Timeline	Right Timeline
Before Retirement Era ending in 1890	1760: Industrial Revolution 1861: U.S. Civil War	1440: Printing Press 1776: United States 1890: Labor Crisis in Germany
Government Supported Forced Retirement Era Abroad (1890-1920)	1914: World War I 1929: Stock Market Crash	Roaring 20's in the U.S. Great Depression
Government Supported Retirement Era in the U.S. (1920-1950)	1935: Social Security Act	World War II
Optional Retirement Era (1950-1980)	Civil Rights Movement 1973: U.S. Off Gold Standard 1975-76: Microsoft & Apple	1969: Moon Landing 1974: IRA Created 1978: 401(k) Created
Expected/Entitled Retirement Era (1980-2010)	1994: Amazon 2000: Dot Com Bubble 2007: The iPhone	1997: Roth IRA Created 2001: 9/11 2007-2009: Housing Financial Crisis
Death of Retirement Era (2010-2040)	Obama Presidency COVID-19 ???	Trump Presidency You Are Here The Future Poor

The period between 1950 and 1980 also was a unique era in retirement history. Prior to that time, people were forced out of work either through incentive, economic collapse, or because they were physically unable to work due to fatigue, health issues, or death. After 1950 the idea of choosing to exit work—with the expectation that things would work out financially for you—became a reality. In less than a century, the Western world had moved from needing to force people out of the workforce to retirement as a voluntary and sustainable choice. This is an important social and economic achievement that should not be understated.

Still, 1950 to 1980 was not a utopia by any stretch of the imagination. From the Civil Rights Movement to the Cold War, Vietnam, Watergate, and the realization that we were collectively poisoning our planet, this period was marked by a series of life-and-death crises. And, even in that golden age of retirement, millions living in the U.S. found optional retirement impossible.

Nevertheless, our view of the world had changed radically from the expectations of Americans before World War II. At the time, five economic and five social factors supported individuals and made a way for millions to cease working at 65. Retirees had their economic needs met. More and more retirement communities began to emerge.

Retirement became an industry.

As of the publication of this book, nearly *$38 trillion* are held in U.S. retirement plans and accounts! And while that may seem like an ocean of money out there to keep us all afloat in the future—our health and well-being in what feels like a successful retirement depends on a whole lot more than money.

6

Exploring the Pillars

By 1980, American culture rested squarely on what I call the Five Economic Pillars of Retirement, which we can summarize as income, expenses, life expectancy, medical needs, and simplicity.

- *Income* was expected to arrive regularly without working.
- *Expenses* were manageable and the cost of living was covered by income.
- *Life expectancy* was lower than today so there were fewer years of life to fund. (Life expectancy remained at about 70 for all Americans through the 1960s and, for men, it did not reach 70 until 1980.)
- *Medical needs* and expenses remained lower in this period.
- *Simplicity* refers to the sense that most people's lives did not vary widely in socioeconomic terms—and that we could get by in relative simplicity in retirement. (It wasn't until 1998 that economist Juliet Schor published her landmark *The Overspent American*, documenting how American expectations of what household "necessities" are had exploded in the late 20th century.)

These Five Economic Pillars of Retirement joined with the Five Social Pillars of Retirement of family, religion, education, government, and corporations to create the sustainable recipe for retirement to be possible. These pillars supported individuals in a way that made optional retirement a reality for people for possibly the first time in human history.

- *Family*, generally the nuclear family, supported one another and provided a launch pad into adulthood.
- *Religious* beliefs and affiliations were high, with 90% of Americans identifying as Christian as recently as the early 1990s.
- *Education* and higher learning took off, with initiatives like the G.I. Bill making way for college. Tuition prices had yet to skyrocket.
- *Government* provided much needed social support and structure.
- *Corporations* provided employment opportunities and, in many cases, lifetime income, through pensions, as a form of loyalty and support.

The Social Determinants of Health

Many years before I began working on *The Future Poor* project, I realized that a "successful" life—a happy life with meaning, purpose, and loved ones around us—somehow revolved around pillars like these ten. That's why my education and professional development has ranged all the way from studying theology and ethics to the practical work of developing financial plans for individuals and major corporations.

All my life, I have known: A good life depends on far more than money.

So, I was thrilled to see the world's public health researchers publishing a whole series of major studies that argue our human happiness—our health and well-being throughout life—depend on a whole series of pillars. They like to call them "determinants." In many ways, this body of research represents another historic change in the way we understand life's stages. Just after 2000, this growing body of public health work became known as the social determinants of health (SDH). According to the World Health Organization (WHO), "The social determinants of health are the non-medical factors that influence health outcomes. They are the conditions in which people are born, grow, work, live, and age, and the wider set of forces and systems shaping the conditions of daily life."

The U.S. Department of Health and Human Services subdivides the SDH into 5 factors:

- Economic stability
- Education access and quality
- Health care access and quality
- Neighborhood and built environment
- Social and community context

Social Determinants of Health

- Income and social protection
- Education
- Unemployment and job insecurity
- Working life conditions
- Food insecurity
- Housing, basic amenities, and the environment
- Early childhood development
- Social inclusion and nondiscrimination
- Structural conflict
- Access to affordable health services of decent quality

As you are reading this chapter, I hope you are connecting the dots with my own lists of retirement "pillars." So, let's keep going—

In 2005, WHO commissioned an extensive report on the SDH that was published in 2008, called "Closing the gap in a generation: Health equity through action on the social determinants of health." The 200-page document outlines the critical importance for every nation around the world to focus on the SDH. Three key actions that frame the report include:

- Improve daily living conditions.
- Tackle the inequitable distribution of power, money, and resources.
- Measure and understand the problem and assess the impact of action.

This global effort is meant to improve all of life, including retirement and the post-productive years of a society's older population. WHO summarizes the critical nature of understanding these underlying pillars of life this way:

> The development of a society, rich or poor, can be judged by the quality of its population's health, how fairly health is distributed across the social spectrum, and the degree of protection provided from disadvantage as a result of ill-health. ... It is essential that governments, civil society, WHO, and other global organizations now come together in taking action to improve the lives of the world's citizens. Achieving health equity within a generation is achievable, it is the right thing to do, and now is the right time to do it.

This call stands at the foundation of why I believe we need to explore and understand these pillars that define our lives—and specifically as you read this book, we need to dive deeper into the pillars that are crucial in shaping our final years. Just as your physical health is not determined by genetics alone, your financial health cannot be reduced to what is in your bank account.

A deeper dive:
The five economic pillars of retirement

The Five
Economic Pillars of Retirement

Income | Expenses | Life Expectancy | Medical Needs | Simplicity

Let's take a look at these five pillars, for I believe they have been the pillars since long before the United States was founded.

Income

For some, this is the obvious first variable. Many call this their "nest egg." I believe the amount of income you can get from that nest egg to be far more important to figure out than how big it is. In other words: The way you are able to *use* what you have accumulated is far more important than *what* you have amassed at the point when you no longer are collecting a regular paycheck.

Income acts as a powerful gauge for us. It may very well be the source of financial anxiety—or potential financial freedom. Of all the anxieties, financial anxiety may be easiest to tie back to an easily quantifiable number since we are dealing with actual dollars and cents. At any given moment we know exactly what our money can buy—or cannot afford. This is very real.

I want to underscore the importance of this very point, as it's often glossed over when I bring it up. When your livelihood and survival is tied to an actual number—in our case, dollars—it can be a terrifying equation. It's a zero-sum game. I have only a certain amount available. If I buy *this*, that means I cannot buy *that*. We are keen observers of this game and we learn to play it very early in life.

I learned it at the age of 10 in the most vivid way imaginable. I was smaller than most kids my age and so were my feet. I was also a lover of basketball. This was 1991 and the birth of the globalization of basketball. One factor in that story was a player by the name of Michael Jordan and his shoes. Perhaps you have heard of him. I wanted to be like Mike. If you're old enough, you probably have the song playing in your head now. I also lived in Portland, Oregon at the time—Nike headquarters. Technically, it's Beaverton, but we think of that as Portland.

My feet were still a bit too small for Air Jordans, so I had to settle for Sky Jordans. My parents were great in that they bought me a cool pair of shoes to start school with, but these were not the same. Today, they make shoes identical. Back then, you could tell. They weren't the same. They didn't have the air pocket. The tiny details were like a bright red blemish on my face.

Over the course of the school year, I grew a bit and saved money. I was 10, so my savings was birthday money, Christmas money, and lawn mowing. At some point in fifth grade, I arrived. My feet required Air Jordans. With my $100 I bought the Air Jordan 6 Infrared. Some of you know. Some of you just Googled that.

I was in heaven—for a couple days.

What happened? These were the greatest things on the planet for a 10-year-old or any shoe enthusiast. But, I found something else I wanted to buy.

And, wearing my Air Jordans, I had no money.

Enter the reality of income in the worst way possible. I remember throwing my shoes at one point while in the garage at our house on Center Street— just days after buying the ultimate purchase of my life.

What did I want to buy instead?

Baseball and basketball cards. I also was a collector of those back in the day. But I had no money so I knew I could not purchase them. My amazing Jordans, which I wore every day and loved to death, were a reminder that the $100 I spent could not be used for anything else because it was in those shoes.

If you've felt some of those feelings yourself—then I have made my point: Income matters—a lot. It mattered when I was 10 and it matters when you and I no longer have a paycheck. Income reveals to us what we can and cannot do every moment of every day. When we are younger, we can look at it and think that we can earn more and work harder. When you are past your working years, the game changes. Money changes for retirees when it shifts from working for income to relying on what you have saved to create your future income.

And remember this: it doesn't matter if you have $100 or $100,000, it depends on what you can actually buy with that money—better known as expenses.

Expenses

Like income, expenses can be a very strange thing when looking at things in two different time periods. When I was growing up, Jordans were one of the first shoes to crack the $100 barrier. Later they would be the first to crack the $200 barrier. Sometimes this matters, sometimes it doesn't. What I mean by that is that expenses are always relative to something else, generally income.

As I write this some 30 years after my Air Jordans purchase, I would love to pay $100 for Jordans. What a deal that would be! And it is not because I am an adult with a job. It is in the relationship to income that expenses get their significance. We have been taught to think of the price of an item as the primary matter. Yet, the cost of something is only relevant in terms of the relationship it has to your income.

This is a thought experiment I have done with a few willing participants. I ask, do you want to buy Jordans for $1,000 or for $100?

What did you pick?

Undoubtedly you picked $100. Why? Because you were thinking of the purchase in relation to your income. Now, let's play the game again and I will give you two different incomes. First, do you want to buy Jordans at $1,000 when your income is $1 million, or do you want to buy Jordans at $100 when your income is $100? The answer is obvious, but is critical in understanding the time and place you are operating in, especially in retirement.

And, even if your income can meet your expenses today—can you continue to meet your expenses years from now? Possibly many years from now!

Life expectancy

Like it or not, we all die.

This shouldn't be a surprise to anyone, but the impact of a long life may be one of the most important variables to any retirement planning. In the

1950s, a retiree at 65 was likely to have only a few more years. Today, life expectancy is far longer.

So, let's try another thought experiment. I am going to give you $1,000 to spend on food. Initially, you'd be happy and grateful—but there is a catch with this one. Is that $1,000 your food budget for seven days—or seven months? If it is seven days, then continue your celebration! But, if that money has to last for seven months, I'm becoming more like a contestant on *Survivor* and treating that money like Jeff Probst has given me a bag of rice I have to make last for 39 days.

This is a danger in retirement that we cannot predict accurately. Two extremes of this equation happened within my own family. When my grandfather retired as a machinist after 40 years in a factory making forklifts, he was ready to exit the workforce and enjoy a simple life of fishing, maybe some travel, and no more factory work. Within a couple of years, a brain tumor took his life. His wife, my Nana, is still alive into her 90s.

How does one plan for a 5-year retirement *and* a 35-year retirement at the same time? How do you make your money last? Fear of running out of money is often cited as the number one fear for retirees.

Making what you have saved last is daunting—but I hope you also are celebrating the astonishing achievements of science over the last century. In the developed world, infant mortality has plummeted compared to previous centuries. The average age of death has been pushed to "old age." Life expectancy has increased by almost two decades in the last century. We keep people alive better than any other point in human history.

That is to be celebrated.

And carefully planned for—to the extent we can.

Medical

As we live longer, the need for medical treatment tends to increase in frequency and severity. Many people have experienced this reality firsthand well before retirement. It can be a crushing financial blow when insurance doesn't cover everything—or there is no insurance at all.

Recently, my son broke his arm. He is young and healthy, but the total cost of this accident was $12,000. The U.S. Census reports that 1 out of 4 American households with children currently have medical debt. Medical debt is the cause of a major portion of personal bankruptcy filings nationwide. This is a serious financial drain for the average citizen and these challenges only increase in frequency and severity as we age.

One of the prevailing myths is that government programs like Medicare are a magic wand that covers all medical needs in retirement. Many retirees are shocked to find that Medicare benefits are limited—much as they are surprised to find that Social Security isn't really income replacement. On top of that, the additional "parts" of Medicare available to expand this coverage are not free. They are better than paying out of pocket for the entire medical expense, but you still need the ability to pay for them.

Elder care and end of life care are the final aspects that can lead to an impoverished retirement and place a financial drag on the family. Plus, to be eligible for certain government benefits, you have to spend down what you have accumulated. Some of the benefits leave the medical options in the hands of the government rather than the freedom of choice for the patient. Caring for a loved one at home is also a financial burden, as well as being physically and emotionally taxing.

On top of all that, there are Medicaid Estate Recovery programs. If you had used Medicaid benefits, Congress mandated that "states must try to recover those expenses from the beneficiaries' estates after their deaths." Your kids or beneficiaries may get a bill from the state to pay back government services that you used.

The last piece of the puzzle deals with the very end of life. A funeral can be an unexpectedly large bill! You may have seen GoFundMe's to help cover a funeral for someone in your circle. How large are these costs? They vary widely and depend on your choices, but the National Funeral Directors Association's latest self-reported data says the median cost nationwide is $8,300. However, that widely reported industry number can be deceptive, because many costs we assume will be part of a funeral can wind up rocketing the cost past $20,000. And remember: All of these expenses could be accrued while the deceased's estate is still being settled, meaning family and friends must pick up the tab in the meantime. Or worse, there are no assets to cover the expense, which is why we see so many GoFundMe's.

Simplicity

Simplicity may seem like an odd economic pillar, but carefully considering this value serves a unique role when thinking about what retirement was, what it is now, and what it could be in the future. In the decades after World War II, economic simplicity made retirement viable—far from the social and economic complexity we inhabit today.

The socioeconomic status of a large portion of our population from 1950 to 1980 was more similar than today. Middle-class incomes were more widespread—and expectations were more limited. Retiring was, well, *simpler* because there was far less stuff to buy, maintain, and replace in our homes.

Economist Juliet Schor's *The Overspent American* drives this point home with devastating simplicity. Her research examined a huge range of consumer products, appliances, and features in homes and cars. With each item, she documents when the product was introduced and when that item became so widespread that these once-new things became absolute "necessities." She defined a "necessity" as something a person is likely to immediately replace or repair if it stops working or is damaged. Most retirees in the 1950s did not expect to own and operate air conditioning systems in their homes, for example. Most retirees in the 1980s did not expect to own a home computer, or a digital printer, or other computer peripherals. Most retirees in 2000 did not expect to own expensive smartphones and pay for expensive service plans. There was no iPhone until 2007. A huge list of "necessities", from microwaves to air fryers to big flat-screen TVs to riding lawn mowers and snow blowers, are all bursting Americans' once far-more-simple retirement budgets.

We need help. And that brings us to—

A deeper dive: The five social pillars of retirement

The Five
Social Pillars of Retirement

Family Religion Education Government Corporations

What will be required of family, religion, education, government, and corporations is a high level of humility and sacrifice to pave a better path to the future.

Family

Family is where it all begins.

For the purposes of understanding the future poor, "family" is a general term referring to adults who were the primary agents in raising us as children—and the deep social network around us we like to call family. Families are varied and each family member can have a unique experience within the same household. They span the socialeconomic landscape, cultural distinctions, geography, and life stages.

One thing that is true of families is they have profound influences upon us.

We adopt and carry forward many of the relational and behavioral patterns we have seen modeled—often more than we care to admit! As we grow up, we keep some of these and discard others. Life and relationships inform which patterns are effective and which are not and then we choose what to do with them.

That's why I like to ask people: "What are some of your earliest memories about money?"

More often than not, common early "money memories" lean towards anxiety and other negative feelings around spending—or that money was never talked about.

"What did your family *teach* you about money?"

I'm asking about basic principles, but many people answer my question with: "Nothing." Others mention general concepts like spending less than you make, avoiding debt and never over drafting your checking account. Very few people describe any specific or tactical financial advice, plans or strategies.

"What did you *learn* about money from your family?"

Children are keen observers. Ask any parent! Ask yourself! You may not have been given any technical money knowledge growing up, but you learned about money by watching the way your family related to and behaved around money.

Questions like these occur in other places where people are concerned about money, our relationships to it, and the things we learn along the way that shape us. *The Art of Money* by Bari Tessler, who works in the financial therapy space, or Tori Dunlap's *Financial Feminist* raise these questions and more to help us understand the foundations of our relationship with money, undoubtedly tied to our family of origin.

Matters of money may be one of the most significant things we learned about growing up without even knowing it. Observing spending patterns taught us what things were important or how to spend money. Tense financial conversations taught us that money's role was both the source of and solution to a multitude of anxieties. Some of us, to this very day, have no idea about the financial situation of our parents. All in all, the sub-50/sub-150 tend to have a similar refrain about money matters in their family: There was not much positive conversation and training happening.

Back in the mid-1970s, young adults were stepping into a world shaped by their parents' generation. Most of the older and simpler financial methods they learned still worked. This led to the greatest accumulation of wealth the world had ever seen for those in the baby boom and early Generation X generations, those born after WWII to 1970. This has also led to the upcoming greatest wealth transfer from generation to generation we have ever seen.

On the face of it, the largest wealth transfer sounds like a great thing and has the potential to be beneficial for some individuals and families. However, the delay in distributing this accumulation to the next generation is another of the most significant ways that the family has backed away from individuals. Today's sub-50/sub-150 ended up on a road to becoming the future poor and in many ways are kept on that path through the lack of earlier distribution of money by their parents.

At this point, I do want to make a couple distinctions to help mend generational miscommunication. The first is between millennial greed versus family economics in the new economy. The economic reality of today for the sub-50 is something quite different than the economic reality of 1980-2010. I describe the current reality as a storm that we have been thrown into and participated in. The previous generations have possessed life jackets and flotation devices this whole time. Maybe they even have a rescue boat! As the typical sub-50 sees their older family members reach for their rescue devices, there is an instinct to beg for saving them, too. Misunderstood, this can be seen as greed, or trying to take the easy path or worse. Money can be seen as both the *source of* and *solution to* financial anxieties and many in the sub-50 are stuck hoping for an inheritance to relieve them from drowning.

How often have you heard lines like—

"You just don't understand what it costs to live today."

"We didn't get any help."

"There's no way to afford that."

"You got yourself into this situation."

"You want help? Do what we did!"

"How do you expect me to get by?"

We should be asking different kinds of questions in our families:

"How can we get out of this cycle of anxiety?"

"How should we be helping each other to build a new financial future?"

Religion and faith communities

Faith matters. So does regular participation in congregations of people who care about each other. That religious pillar of our lives is a predictor of health and well-being as we age.

That's the conclusion of 20 years of research into the SDH around the world. Scientists studying the SDH are not arguing that is due to divine intervention or that one particular religious group has an inside track on health. But, there now is solid, secular research showing that a connection with a faith community contributes to our overall health and longevity.

Some of these findings follow common sense. For example, we know that isolation and exclusion are well-documented predictors of declining health. In contrast, faith communities regularly remind us that we are not alone. Plus, many congregations provide practical help through their caregiving networks, especially when people are facing crises. In fact, all of the world's major religious traditions encourage helping each other. That's why the Vatican has been actively working with the World Health Organization in promoting the SDH—and other religious groups are doing the same.

In graduate school, when I studied ancient Israel, I learned that connections between religious, legal, and economic matters were paramount to the establishment of a nation. To this day, Jewish communities around the world pay particular attention to sharing resources in times of need—and Jews certainly are not alone. To some extent, every major religious denomination in the U.S. includes outreach programs to help both members and people living far beyond their home communities.

The United States was founded as a blend of individualism, capitalism, democracy, and assumptions about the Christian faith. While the faith intentions of our founding fathers are hotly debated by historians, they did achieve an approach to religion that was unique in the world: Americans are free to practice any form of religion—and also are supposed to be free from any state influence on behalf of religion: "freedom to" and "freedom from." Historians credit that founding concept with producing one of the most religiously active—and most religiously diverse—nations in the world.

During the post-WWII economic expansion and the rise of the middle class, there was a parallel shift in American religiosity and church life. Congregations boomed along with the entire American economy.

Having been raised within the American Evangelical Christian tradition, I got to see this shift firsthand and was an active participant in several growing churches in different parts of the U.S. The idea of a megachurch did not exist prior to the 1970s, but today they are everywhere. Some smaller churches were replaced by massive highly organized and heavily resourced churches. This encouraged new models of celebrity pastors—a cultural movement that Robert Reich calls, "paying for stars."

Churches large and small have become active participants in marketing, branding, and competing for attendees and their money. While the shape, size, and even the definitions of American Christianity are shifting dramatically since the COVID pandemic, there still are more than 350,000 congregations in the U.S. Even though the majority of houses of worship across the U.S. are small—most have less than 100 active members—our faith communities still can do a great deal to shape our collective ethical transformation toward helping each other in important ways.

Don't take my word for it, if you are skeptical of this message coming from a person of faith. One of the most famous advocates for developing new sustainable communities around the world is James Gustav Speth, a secular scholar who co-founded the National Resources Defense Council and has headed up a long list of international cooperative efforts to save at-risk communities. Speth was acting on SDH principles around the world years before there was such a thing as the SDH. In a series of books—written from his perspective as a nonbeliever himself—he has urged the world's major faith communities to work together to help preserve lives and change the course of our global climate crisis. In fact, he argues that we can't save our planet's population without the active participation of faith leaders. Speth argues that no other global organizations have the particular moral authority of religions to help people reshape their lives in the dramatic ways necessary to turn around many of the troubling trends in our world. "The potential of faith communities is enormous—and they are turning more attention to issues of social justice, peace and environment," he writes.

Well, to qualify Speth's optimism, it's clear: Some faith communities are. Some are not. Some are becoming more insular and contributing to the isolationism and exclusion that run counter to public health and well-being.

In my freshman year of college, I took a world religions class. The professor was an atheist but, like Speth, he argued that for the good of the world, we all need to learn more about our global faith traditions. His perspective impressed me from the first day of class. He was older and carried himself as one with wisdom, experience, and humility. He began the class by disclosing that he was an atheist, but that we should not confuse the content of the course with his own beliefs. Second, he instructed us that we would not spend any time debating the things we do not like about religion. What we were going to do was study the major world religions with a focus on teachings that might continue to have value in our world.

Consider a few of the questions he asked us:

"Do you believe in helping the poor?"

"Should we do unto others as we would have them do to us?"

"How are you doing following those teachings?"

It's easy to pick apart the things we do not like about religious institutions, but his call was to something more human, more ethical, more universal.

He wanted us to pause and really think.

Religion has and always will be part of the social fabric of the world. Among the hallmarks of religious history are the establishment of hospitals, orphanages, and other institutions to care for the world's most vulnerable. To this day, a majority of hospitals across the U.S. have a faith group in their founding stories. And, for their part, thousands of congregations nationwide continue to care for the vulnerable in many ways. But, I wonder: Are they ready for the much greater focus on such values needed in the years ahead?

Such a focus requires the humility needed to move outward rather than inward and shift financial resources in large ways toward these outward efforts. As I look at the landscape of my own evangelical religious tradition, to the extent money is talked about at all, I continue to be troubled by two unhelpful extremes. One is the ongoing "prosperity movement" among some televangelists who claim that gifts to the church will result directly in blessings from God—a message that also tries to justify lavish spending by those very preachers and their families. Another is a tendency in congregations to talk about money only when annual fundraising appeals roll around.

Too few pastors in the U.S. are courageous enough to preach about the need to radically rethink the way we share our resources that is urged by major figures like Speth or Pope Francis—or even Jesus himself in the Gospels, for that matter.

Those of us who care about our churches need to study our Bibles more seriously—as well as significant books and teaching materials about economic life that are already available. It is indeed true that the Bible speaks more about money than any other single moral issue in this world. These biblical teachings need to be considered, in their entirety and in their complexity. It helps to see how moral thinkers have sifted through these materials to develop coherent bodies of teaching. I have seen excellent Protestant, Catholic, and Eastern Orthodox materials that are available to congregations—if lay leaders and clergy look for them, read them, and discuss them with others. These teachings all avoid the magical thinking that is the prosperity gospel; and, while they acknowledge that wealth can become an idol, they also teach that every person needs enough resources to meet their needs and the needs of those for whom they are responsible—and that God intends that this be possible for each person. Church leaders need to do their homework to study these kinds of resources and then to present them in practical ways to their congregants. And I can add from research that such resources exist, as well, in the best of Jewish, Muslim, Buddhist, and Hindu traditions, as well.

This call is so central to Christian teaching and most other prominent faith traditions and is something I hope we all take seriously.

In fact, Speth puts it this way: "Full of hope, it is time to rise up and make history."

I agree.

Education

Education's influence takes on several forms and isn't strictly intellectual. For most of us, education is one of the first open doors to the world outside our families. We are exposed to information, ideas, and people outside of our home. Social development expands. Subjects start to shape interests. Other influences open our eyes to a broader world. All of this happens during the most formative stages of human development and that is why it is so important.

Like most of you, I was strongly influenced by men and women I met at school. For me, a major standout was a professor, Dr. David Gushee. In my junior year as an undergraduate, I took his Approaches to Moral Decision Making course, which turned out to be a dramatic turning point. After only one class, Dr. Gushee inspired me to change my major. I have remained in touch with Dr. Gushee through the years and, as I was drafting this book, he graciously read an early manuscript and helped with the editing. That's just one example of my education truly shaping my life. This is education's "magic" layered on top of intellectual and social development. Educators are content deliverers, content creators, and mind shapers, and must be considered a critical component in making a significant shift in the conversation around the future poor.

While some teachers—or other school professionals like counselors or coaches—can play dynamic roles in our lives, the curriculum itself changes at a glacial pace. As my oldest children are entering middle school and high school, I have been watching what they are learning, and it is essentially a repeat of what I learned 30 years previous. Some world and U.S. history, learning the presidents in order, reading and writing, and the basics of science and math. One thing that is missing in all of this is any education around money and economics. It was missing in my day, and it is still not present.

We can intuit that money is important, maybe one of the most important parts of life to understand. Yet, money management has been avoided or placed somewhere outside of most public school curricula that I have seen. There may be some discussion of money as examples in math courses and perhaps there's an elective home economics course offered for high school students. In my experience, I recall one week devoted to the study of money management out of my four years of high school.

And, as a general rule, it's easy to earn a college degree without any course work devoted to financial issues—unless you are enrolled in specific business and management courses, that is. There are some excellent business and entrepreneurial courses at universities nationwide—but, in recent years, popular culture seems to have celebrated the irrelevance of higher education for successful entrepreneurs. Millions of Americans know that Steve Jobs, Bill Gates, Michael Dell, and Mark Zuckerberg all dropped out of college.

One truth we know about higher education is: Nothing in the U.S. has inflated quite like the cost of a college degree. According to the National Center for Education Statistics, since 1980, the cost of college tuition, fees, books, and room and board has grown by more than 200%. That's more than two times that of the overall consumer price index for all goods! In many ways, our system of higher education—and its enormous funding network from student loans—looks a lot like a "get rich quick" scheme for those institutions pocketing all that money from millions of students. Student loan debt now amounted to over $1.7 trillion dollars at the time I write this, with many feeling like there is no way out of this pit.

How does student debt relate to the later-in-life crisis of the future poor? For most of the sub-50/sub-150 population, our origin story includes this crushing debt—along with that gap in addressing money math in most of our school years.

My daughter asked me recently why she doesn't learn money math in school. She was frustrated! She knew that what she called "money math" could be a valuable asset in her life. "And when am I ever going to need to know the area of a triangle as an adult?!" she complained.

I did not have a good answer.

Government

Government's influence in some ways overshadows the other pillars.

Consider: The elementary school you attended, and where your children may now be enrolled, has very little influence on the company where you are employed—but the government influences both. Its influence was there before you and I were born and will be around long after we are gone.

This significant influence leads directly to the primary functions of government—to advance the common good and to legislate for the purpose of maintaining the values of our constitutional republic. In its simple form, the government is to be both carrot and stick for the betterment of its citizens and country.

This presents a unique burden on the government. It is not the responsibility of the government to solve this crisis alone. A true democracy never leaves everything at the feet of its elected officials. Still, since so many policies related to retirement reside in the hands of our government, its activities must be taken seriously.

Many states, along with the federal government, have started making inroads with certain aspects of this issue.

Washington state, for example, initiated a mandatory "long-term care" tax for all W2 employees in order to fund a state long-term care benefit to help offset the cost of senior care. A dozen other states have begun to pursue a similar course.

My home state of California passed a law requiring employers with more than five workers to provide mandated retirement plans or alternatively to enroll each of their people in a state-run retirement plan and auto-deduct 5% from employees' paychecks. Soon this law will expand to include anyone with an employee.

At the time of this book's publication, legislation continues to be debated at the federal level to mandate retirement options for all businesses, which could be a positive step. At least the debate shows some concern in Washington about the ominous cliff we are approaching. But most proposals involve sticks—mandates, taxes, and penalties—rather than carrots. Those sticks clash with Americans' deep assumptions that government should be about protecting freedoms—like speech, religion, opportunity, life, liberty, and property. Clearly, government has a major role to play, but—as of this writing—I cannot see any governmental solution for the future poor popping up. Keep reading, because I am calling for us to realize we have a collective responsibility, but I am also being honest here: I cannot see how our government can solve such a complicated and multilayered ethical challenge with a singular and simple solution.

Corporations

The landscape of work has radically transformed over the past 50 years and these changes are accelerating every day. No doubt technology's advancement played a major role. But, if technology was the engine, then the move away from the gold standard was the fuel. This shift allowed access to money to match the speed of business and was critical in making the world we live in today.

Another major shift began to occur within the corporate world. Prior to 1978, many companies handled retirement through pensions. Pensions came in all shapes and sizes. To this day, many of those plans are not complete income replacements. However, corporations sold their employees on the idea that if you worked a long career, then the company would take care of you by giving you a monthly paycheck when you retired. Almost two-thirds of companies still provided these plans in 1980.

So what happened in 1978? That was the advent of the 401(k), something most of us are familiar with and think of as the primary retirement savings account. The advent of the 401(k), which is named after a section of the federal tax code, brought about a radical shift for corporations and employees. This was great for companies, but I am skeptical how great it has been for employees. This shift and the continual move away from pensions—only about 4% of companies offer them anymore—is the key movement away from individuals that companies made in regard to retirement.

I realize you might be saying, "But I love my 401(k) and I am so glad to have it!"

Sure! We should be grateful for them. But the sub-50 generation has no real comparison since that's all we've had as adult workers. What we need to understand more clearly is why the 401(k) came about and how it massively changed the financial game for businesses—especially publicly traded companies. First, we need to understand how company valuations look at their balance sheets. On one side are assets. On the other are liabilities. More assets and less liabilities equal greater corporate value.

A pension is an obligation to pay and sits on the liabilities side of the business. For many companies, it was their largest liability. As people live longer that obligation only becomes bigger and bigger. Think of it as a huge ball and chain tied around the company's neck. This was not good for corporate America.

On the other hand, a 401(k) does not show up on the liabilities side of the spreadsheet. It actually works like an asset for a company since there is no obligation other than a possible corporate match to the employee's contribution—and it is a tax write-off for the business. Companies with large pensions cannot show the type of profitability they may like, the cash flow and reserves they may like, or be valued as highly because of the large obligation. That is why corporations were so eager to abandon pensions.

However, they could never completely eliminate a benefit without an alternative—or the workforce would rebel.

So, in the 1970s there was work done to create an alternative type of account that served the purpose of providing for retirement but did away with the liability. And in 1978 we got the 401(k).

The timing of this came right before the Reagan administration of the 1980s. The stock market entered into American culture and consciousness in ways it never had before. Stock price, valuation, and growth all followed. For example, the S&P 500 was around $100 in 1980. Businesses needed to be ready for the new world of the American and global economy or be left behind. Corporations needed to dump liabilities and the largest one was often the pension.

I do not want to be completely negative about this shift. In general, pensions had to go away because they did not fit the new economy ushered in by the 1980s. The days of getting a job as early as age 18 and never leaving a company until retirement was part of the old world. We soon needed, and still require, a portable retirement system. The 401(k) makes that available when combined with individual retirement arrangements, or IRAs, which began a few years earlier in 1974. Currently, people are changing jobs every two to five years, and it's estimated that people just entering the workforce now will have five or six careers, while those on the older end of the sub-50 will have about three changes. This has only accelerated in the past decade and will continue. In addition to that, the rise of the "gig economy" requires individuals to set up their own futures, since we are all becoming less and less dependent upon corporations for our future.

When you put this all together, it is easy to see why corporations have moved further and further away from playing a significant role in an employee's retirement.

The key mistake most people make in trusting their 401(k)s to take care of their future is: A retirement account is never a substitute for a **retirement plan**. Complicating matters is the common sub-50 assumption that simply having a 401(k) guarantees a smooth retirement.

While I do not believe that corporations are doing nearly enough to help their employees plan for retirement—I also do not lay the entire responsibility at their feet. My hope is that they will use their enormous, collective financial strength to become a greater part of the solution.

Media

Yes, this would seem to be the sixth area in a section limited to five pillars—but we cannot finish our tour of those pillars without considering how media shapes our assumptions of the Big Five.

"Financial television" did not really exist until 1989, when CNBC began broadcasting 24 hours of information about the stock market, business, and other financial news. Subsequent channels sprouted as we moved into the 1990s. And now? Just try to escape it! The stock market is everywhere, as if it is the single financial metric that matters. From there, we move to the apps and platforms that facilitate trading for retail investors (individuals outside the financial professional world). Most of those employ the very same psychological and physiological techniques as Las Vegas casinos.

If that were not enough, our TikTok and Instagram feeds continue to send us "magical social media financial advice." Every day and everywhere, we get messages extolling owning 10 Airbnbs, only traveling in your private G5 airplane, or that if you don't own a Bugatti you're doing it wrong. This further complicates our relationship with money and drives us further away from psychological and financial well-being.

I see media and social media as a vapor, filling in a void left by the Big Five rather than being of the same socioeconomic substance as family, religion, or the government. While it does possess significant influence, we may have given it more credit than it deserves. I do not believe it can actually produce what the five pillars have the power and potential to do.

Media is not a practical partner like the five pillars, which is why I do not believe it to be a primary focus area for the remedy of the future poor scenario. At best, it is a secondary focus area to be used to highlight the unfortunate changes being made by the five pillars. In building toward how to solve this crisis, I think of the story Jesus told of a man building his house on sand. When storms came, his home failed because it was not built on a solid foundation. Media is sand. Media will be needed, but not for building anew. "The Five" is the rock I wish to build solutions on.

But, before moving on to figuring out what we can do to change our trajectory, there is one more surprise ahead.

7

Let's Play *The Game of Life*

Americans have been playing versions of Milton Bradley's *The Game of Life* since 1860—so we should be pretty good at it, right?

In the version of the board game sub-50 Americans grew up playing, we spin our way through the game, collect blue and pink people-pegs, draw a card to discover our career, hit bumps along the way—and eventually we learn the value of all that effort in the famous "Day of Reckoning."

So, let's give it a whirl!

How'd you do?

Pretty good?

Did you beat your competitors? Hopefully! Perhaps you were playing with your kids on a random weekday night, maybe you have a competitive edge in some ways because you have a little more life under your belt. *The Game of Life* is about acquiring more points and money than your competitors. Some of the outcome is pure luck, but there's a lot of strategy involved as well.

So, how'd you do?

You won! Great work. Fold the board and put the cards, people-pegs, cars, and everything else in the box and bask in family game night glory.

Now, how about your real-life Day of Reckoning? You made it to the end of the real game of life. You are now retired from work and ready to enjoy your twilight years.

But wait, we have some surprises!

First, does the real-life game measure your victory against opponents?

Not at all. This is a different type of game.

Perhaps your own Day of Reckoning is due to luck—perhaps to strategic planning. But I can tell you this real-life game doesn't end at retirement. Nope. This is simply a doorway to the next level of the game—and there are new challenges that weren't in the original instructions.

Consider this phase two of *The Game of Life*—a type of "welcome to retirement" gift, but not something you really want. The surprise comes as the unexpected gift of extra costs and taxes, something no one lets you know is waiting for you at the end of the game. We think the game of life ends at 65 or a final square that simply reads "retirement." It is so much easier to calculate your winnings at the end of a board game!

When you step into the rest of the real-life game, you get a couple bonuses: Social Security and Medicare. Yippee! Your income and medical expenses are covered in the next round! What more could you ask for? But make sure you read the fine print about these benefits, because there are twists and turns you may not have anticipated—like extra taxes and expenses.

What?!

No!

You reach for a copy of the rules and suddenly realize you missed a tiny little asterisk at the end of the instructions. That asterisk links to the fine print instructing you to go online to an obscure website to learn much, much more.

Most of us were so focused on the fun of accumulation that we didn't give much thought to this second phase. So, let me guide you through a couple of the key rules that I believe you want to know before entering into the real-life retirement phase of this game.

Social Security

This is the first part of the retirement journey. You've been paying into it during your working years and now it's time to collect your replacement income. Surprise! It is not a replacement income and not even close.

Here's another action item: A previous action item was to go on ssa. gov and make an account. This action item is to look at the fine print. As I was completing this book, one of my good friends noticed a little section on his statement that said, "The Social Security Board of Trustees estimates that, based on current law, the Trust Funds will be able to pay benefits in full and on time until 2034. In 2034, Social Security would still be able to pay about $800 for every $1,000 in benefits scheduled."

He was floored.

We have had this idea that Social Security is supposed to do more—and it used to. In that 1950–1980 window it was more effective because the cost-of-living side of life after 65 was close to the level of income coming in from this benefit. Life expectancy was also less, so the overall fund had to pay for less years. That is not the case today and people are starting to figure it out. Social Security used to be one of the big three income supports for retirees. Now it is shockingly low compared to our former income and current cost of living.

Will it be there when you retire? That could be another surprise. You have probably seen doomsday reports about the federal government running out of money to finance the system. That may happen—but I do not believe the program will go away. Nearly everyone in Washington D.C. knows that cutting Social Security amounts to political suicide. More likely: The system will adjust and morph into something else. Right now about 20% of federal spending each year goes towards Social Security checks for retirees. That is a huge percentage and a number that millions depend upon nationwide. As the situation progresses, and more and more people retire with fewer and fewer personal resources, public programs like this will be all the more important.

Unfortunately, Social Security is likely to disappoint your expectations.

To give you a little perspective on what Social Security checks look like for people, here are a couple reference points. I encourage you to apply them to your situation and see what you think.

According to the ssa.gov FAQs page, "The estimated average amount changes monthly. For example, the estimated average monthly Social Security retirement benefit for January 2024 is $1,907." That is $22,884 a year—just a few thousand over the federal poverty level numbers.

If you make $75,000 a year, your Social Security will be about $28,000/year.

If you make $100,000 a year, you should expect about $34,000/year.

Roughly speaking, at most, and if everything goes right—and you wait to take your benefits until one of the older ages built into the system—your Social Security may replace about one-third of your income. That's a start, but it certainly isn't income replacement. Your Social Security Statement even includes this:

> Important Things to Know about Your Social Security Benefits
>
> Social Security benefits are not intended to be your only source of retirement income. You may need other savings, investments,

pensions, or retirement accounts to make sure you have enough money when you retire.

Are you ready for the next surprise?

When you go to request your benefit and start taking your Social Security, you may want to fill out IRS Form W-4V so that they can withhold federal income tax from your Social Security benefit.

"Wait. What?!"

I can imagine your expression as you read that statement. Your head swiveled. Your eyes widened. Your eyebrows raised. You are puzzled, thinking: "Really? No, that can't be right."

But look at what it says when you visit: irs.gov/forms-pubs/about-form-w-4-v "If you receive any government payment shown below (Social Security), you may use this form to ask the payer to withhold federal income tax."

Did you know that your Social Security is subject to federal income tax?

I have yet to find any sub-50 who understands this looming challenge.

"Income tax? How is the tax that I have paid now subject to income tax?!"

Trust me, I am with you, and had the same shock at this realization. No one has thought that it makes sense, but there it is: The U.S. government looks at your earnings and income, even after retirement, even Social Security, and taxes based on that.

Up to 85% of your Social Security can be subject to income tax. The following comes directly from the Social Security site, www.ssa.gov.

If you file a federal tax return as an individual and your combined income is ...

- between $25,000 and $34,000, you may have to pay income tax on up to 50 percent of your benefits.
- more than $34,000, up to 85 percent of your benefits may be taxable.

If you file a joint return, and you and your spouse have a combined income that is ...

- between $32,000 and $44,000, you may have to pay income tax on up to 50 percent of your benefits.
- more than $44,000, up to 85 percent of your benefits may be taxable.

But wait, there are more surprises! From the FAQ page of the ssa.gov site:

You can get Social Security retirement benefits and work at the same time. However, if you are younger than full retirement age and make more than the yearly earnings limit, we will reduce your benefit.

By now you are probably thinking: Why even bother? Just keep my money!

If you take your benefit before full retirement age of 67 and you have earned income coming in, the government will start to reduce your benefit. If you work in retirement and make $21,240, they will start to deduct $1 of your benefit for every $2 you make over that.

For example, let's say you work a part-time job to support yourself in retirement and you make $30,000, or $8,760 more than the limit. For every $2 over the limit, they take $1. Your benefit will be reduced by $4,380.

The potential problem for those in the sub-50 age bracket with this particular example is that the full retirement age changes. It used to be 65. Then it became 67. That little change 40 years ago saved money by cutting benefits by 13%. We do not know what the Social Security age limits will be in 20 years, but this is not likely to be a good scenario for us.

This once foundational piece of the retirement landscape has quickly become a complicating factor for the middle class. Social Security certainly is no remedy for financial stability in retirement.

Medicare

What do you know about Medicare?

The general idea among most sub-50s I know is that it is free medical care when you're done working. But, by now you may be getting the keen sense that this is another surprise—and you would be right.

Broadly speaking, Medicare is a government program that provides for your medical expenses after your working years. But, did you know that it is not free? Do you know what Part C is? Probably not.

What most Americans don't know is that we need to combine Medicare with private insurance to fill in the gaps. Simply put, Medicare is four parts and only one is free—for most people. Each part does something different, yet all four parts are not comprehensive even when put together.

Part A, the free one, is considered hospital insurance.

Part B is Medicare insurance and you'll pay a premium for coverage every month. Guess what? This is deducted from your Social Security benefit every month. Surprise!

Part C is the gap insurance that you get from private insurance providers that offer these plans. The cost depends on the provider and plan that you pick. These will also vary in what they cover that Part A and B do not.

Part D is for prescription drug coverage.

Yes, it's time for an action item: To learn more about what to expect, check out the hhs.gov site of the U.S. Department of Health and Human Services.

The most significant gap in Medicare is how it handles any sort of skilled nursing facility that you may need. This is one of the most expensive costs for older people and one of the most limited benefits provided by Medicare. Most people are shocked to find that Medicare only covers 20 days. In days 21 – 100, Medicare will pay for things that exceed your deductible. After day 100, you are on your own! The lesson here is to make sure that if you need to be in a skilled nursing facility, make sure you only do it for three months.

Are you confident that you will be able to arrange that?

A study prepared by the U.S. Department of Health and Human Services (HHS), Office of Disability, Aging and Long-Term Care Policy (DALTCP) and the Urban Institute focused on the question, "What is the lifetime risk of needing and receiving long-term services and supports (LTSS)? The answer included the phrase: "70% of people who survive to age 65 will have severe needs for LTSS before they die."

Retirement overlaps with other significant social issues, like gender inequality. If you are a woman reading this, you are more likely to need this type of care and so preparing for it is important. Women need care longer (3.7 years) than men (2.2 years).

2020 U.S. Census data reveals what we all intuit, women live longer than men. By age 92, women outnumber men 2 to 1. This is also the case in nursing homes, with higher percentages of women needing nursing home care after age 75 than men. Of the almost 1.5 million people currently in nursing homes, 70% are women.

A widespread assumption is that government programs will take care of our final needs. This is partially true—but it often requires spending all or most of your assets, generally excluding your house, before you can be eligible to meet the criteria for public assistance. And the government looks back several years to make sure you didn't get rid of a bunch of money in order to qualify. At this point, the state directs and selects your stay and care. Should you wish to select your facility, or your family would like you in a better place, you or your family will need to pay out of pocket for it.

In fact, Medicare is up front about the challenges, warning us: "Medicare and most health insurance, including Medicare Supplement Insurance (Medigap), don't pay for long-term care."

How enormous are these costs? According to the National Council on Aging, the national average for a private room in a facility that provides skilled nursing care is $9,034 a month, or $108,408 a year. The following chart outlines the costs for different levels of senior care. In most cases, the more care we need, the greater the cost. And these are in today's dollars as I complete this book—not future dollars where the amount needed will only be greater.

Type of Care	Monthly Average
Home health aide	$4,957
Adult day center	$1,600
Assisted living facility	$4,500
Memory care	$6,160
Nursing home, shared room	$7,908
Nursing home, private room	$9,034

Credit: © National Council on Aging. Information reprinted with permission. All rights reserved. From: https://www.ncoa. org/adviser/local-care/assisted-living/costs/

This leaves aged people and their loved ones in a medically complicated and financially untenable situation. Should you require more than even one year in this situation, you are now looking at hundreds of thousands of dollars that most people's nest eggs are not equipped to handle. Finally, stop to consider for a moment: Twenty percent of these older folks need more than 5 years of care!

Taxes

This is the final surprise waiting for us in retirement. One of the most influential treatments that I have seen on this issue is called *The Tax Bomb in Your Retirement* by Josh Scandlen. This book is powerful and eye-opening.

We think that no longer having a job means no longer having taxes. Or, we will have less income so we will have little or no taxes. Sometimes this is the case, but it doesn't take much income to generate a tax liability. And did you know that the higher the income coming in—the higher your Medicare cost can be?

Income coming in also can move you into higher tax brackets situations than you may have been expecting. For example, most people have been deferring their taxes in their retirement accounts with the idea that they will be paying less taxes in retirement. In fact, it's likely you will end up paying more taxes in total through this method. The complicating factor is that all your benefits and resources available to you are based on your taxable income and we have been building up large tax liabilities as we save in our 401(k)s and IRAs.

What percentage of your 401(k) is actually yours? This is a question I ask people to get them thinking about their future tax situation.

My general assumption as I talk to people is that about 25% of tax-deferred accounts represent a tax transfer, tax holding, and tax growth investment for the government that you fund, not save.

- Tax transfer means that the taxes your employer owed got sent to your 401(k).
- Tax holding is that you still owe taxes on the money you moved to your account.
- Tax growth means that when you go to use your account, any of the growth will be taxed.

When we begin to withdraw money to fund our retirement needs, we must pay the taxes we have been deferring and growing. If you need a low level of income from your accounts, you may not pay much in taxes. If you need $50,000 or $100,000, you may be paying 20–25% of it in taxes in addition to paying tax on your Social Security and affecting your Medicare costs.

And there's more! Don't forget about taxes at the state level, too. At the time of writing this, 43 states charge income tax and tax retirement income in various ways. Twelve states charge you state income tax on your Social Security benefit. Plus, if you own a home, you have to keep in mind property taxes, another complex issue with laws that vary widely state by state.

"What in the world?!" is what I can imagine you are thinking right now. Early in the book you exclaimed "Too much math!" and now this. "How are we supposed to know all this and figure it out?!"

I know! It is a lot.

All of these factors amount to a delicate and complicated balancing act—and most sub-50s barely know the rules of this game, let alone all of the fine print.

All of this, sadly, reinforces my concern that many of us are on a path toward the future poor.

8

Reimagining the Road to Success and Failure

Welcome to the midpoint of this book, a metaphorical fork in the road both in the content and in the direction of our journey together. Where I live in the Pasadena, California area, we have a real, 18-foot-tall fork standing on a small patch of grass at a divide on a highly trafficked street. Driving by that fork many times has started me thinking of its deeper meaning.

Our gigantic fork has four tines and the fork I want you to consider next has four options: We can turn around and run back to where we started. We can stop moving. Or we can keep going on one of the two roads that are opening up ahead of us.

As we pause for a moment at that big fork, you may be asking some of the most common questions I hear from friends, colleagues, and clients. They often start, "I hear what you're saying, but isn't this whole thing just—

- A personal savings problem?
- A lack of work ethic problem?
- A spending on unnecessary items problem?
- A credit card usage problem?
- A failure to be able to buy a home?

In addition to that common list, I've also heard about other possible culprits like debt, student loans, and our general consumer culture. Behind these responses is the idea that you could fix your retirement challenge by fixing one or two dumb things you are doing. I believe this is both too simplistic and ultimately unhelpful. Certainly, we should consider the things on this list. I work with many of my clients on those behavioral issues and I have had to work on them myself. Reckless spending and overuse of credit cards is a real problem.

But such behaviors do not exist in a vacuum. More importantly, by focusing on that list above, we are dumping a complicated national problem on the shoulders of individuals.

I love a good 2-by-2 matrix, so I designed one for us to use in this conversation. I have found this helpful with colleagues and clients as well.

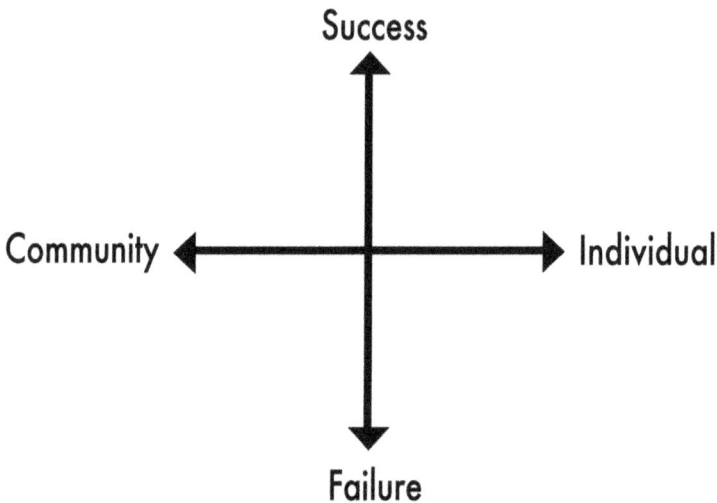

In the World War II era, we looked at America primarily through the lens of community and success. We won. We defeated the Nazis. We became the primary superpower in the world. We did it.

But now, we tend to look at everything as an individual failure or success. Our sense of community has evaporated.

Think about these common assumptions:

- Credit card debt: individual failure
- Do not own a home: individual failure
- Lack of retirement savings: individual failure
- Bezos, Musk, and Buffett: individual success
- Michael Jordan, Kobe Bryant, Tom Brady, or your favorite athlete: individual success
- Your neighbor with the large house and fancy car: individual success

- A person you know who made money on the GameStop short squeeze of 2021: individual success

Several of my personal heroes are coaches Bill Belichick, Mike Krzyzewski, Gregg Popovich, Phil Jackson, and Nick Saban. These five have won more basketball and football championships over the last 30 years than any other coaches. In fact, they all have won five or more since the 1990s. This is something unparalleled in the realm of men's collegiate and professional football and basketball.

Where do you think these people would place themselves on the 2-by-2 matrix? Read on!

My basic chart may look simple—but now we are realizing that it poses some very difficult questions. When we come to matters of poverty in America, most of us don't know where to place our "dot" on the matrix. We certainly do not think of poverty as a community or individual *success*. The problem of poverty obviously is too widespread for that. But we aren't entirely able to call poverty exclusively a *community* failure. Most of us are willing to acknowledge that in a country as rich as ours, desperate poverty must have strong social or community roots. As income levels rise, though, our assumptions move closer to the right in this chart. Individuals with higher incomes should be able to do something about their own situations, shouldn't they?

When we do talk about retirement planning, we say things like: Take personal responsibility! You need to save! You need to max out your 401 (k)! If not: You are the problem!

Yet, we're full of ambivalence about this fork in the road. Not all of us are able to save. Those who take community context seriously see systematic access barriers to retirement. And yet, we also like to claim some community pride in successes. When we see a rich family passing wealth to the next generation, we admire and perhaps envy them. We want to be part of that community success—and would like them to share some of their wealth with us! Wealth creates wealth. We understand this but part of us doesn't respect that truth on a deeper level. We tend to admire people who work for their financial success more than those who are born with a silver spoon.

But widespread poverty? The future poor? This is a looming crisis too big to rely on our old assumptions. We need to think in fresh ways—together.

What if we were to think differently in regard to our 2-by-2 matrix? Remember my question: Where do you think my coaching heroes Bill Belichick, Mike Krzyzewski (Coach K), Gregg Popovich (Pop), Phil Jackson, and Nick Saban would place themselves? I have followed them, watched the documentaries, read the books, and have seen most of the sporting events they have participated in over the last several decades. So, here's how I would answer that question.

Duke and Coach K were dominant in the '90s, but his teams would go on to win in three different decades—almost unheard of in major sports. My other coaching heroes did similar feats, but none would say they did it alone.

Belichick was forever paired with Tom Brady. Phil Jackson had Michael Jordan, Scottie Pippen, Dennis Rodman, Shaquille O'Neal, and Kobe Bryant. Pop had David Robinson, Tim Duncan, and a number of other basketball greats. Each also had his unique coaching system. They had management and organizations that believed in them. They all won in very different decades and evolutions of their sport. All these championships, awards, and successes could not be summed up as simply placing a dot on the 2-by-2 of individual success.

No, something more important was going on in their lives and I believe there is a lesson for us to learn about finances that extends far beyond a point on the matrix.

What if the matrix was built in a different way? Rather than a single dot situated in only one quadrant, what if there were a variety of dots in all four quadrants? What if only a percentage of my favorite coaches' success was attributed to their own efforts? What if our successes were the same, only partially due to our own efforts?

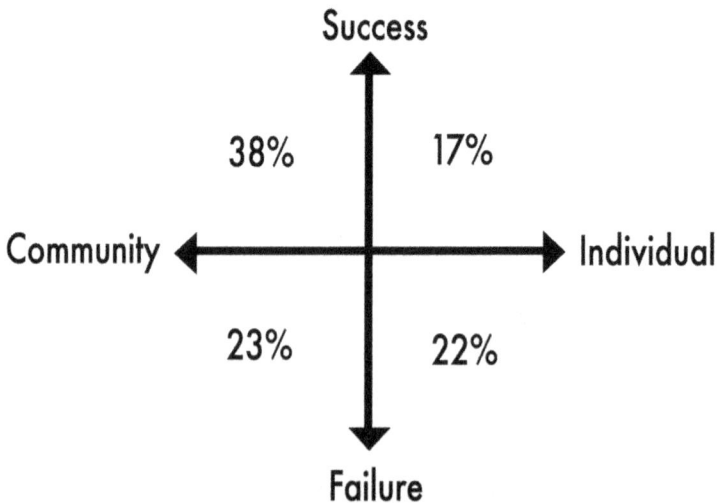

The complexity of winning a championship is akin to the complexity of financial progress. It takes recognizing all the factors that create a winning recipe and keen awareness of the things that prevent progress toward the goal. Perhaps only 17% of your financial situation are your successes. Following this approach, we begin to see that these factors are interconnected and the whole picture is a lot more complicated than one dot.

Would this represent reality more accurately?

And would this present us with a better framework for approaching financial matters in our current context?

Remember that giant fork in the road—the one with four tines?

Would this final percentage-based matrix—in which we can think about using all four quadrants—ease some of the anxiety and frustration felt by each of us?

I think so.

Certainly, we are facing a major fork in the road—but what if, before barreling on down the road, we pause to explore all the directions and resources around us?

9

Why Feel Sorry for the Middle Class?

I am not naïve. In talking with thousands of people over the years, I realize that it's hard to work up much sympathy for people earning $100,000 a year in that sub-150 group that concerns me so much, when millions are making far less. What's more—we all know that the higher end of the sub-150 have many of their daily needs taken care of than people making far less money.

In fact, I don't want you to feel sorry for people who have cracked six figures in their income. I don't even want you to feel sorry for the millions who are likely to become the future poor. It's not that I lack compassion—it's that feeling sorry for someone is seldom a powerful enough motivator for making major changes.

And there's another reason I'm not asking you to feel sorry about any particular group of wage earners: I do not believe there is an absolute correlation between higher earnings and a better life—or long-term well-being.

Remember my earlier chapter about life's pillars and the relatively new global understanding of the social determinants of health? Certainly, "economic stability" is the first of the five major SDH factors listed by our U.S. Department of Health and Human Services. And money is necessary in this country to pay for the next two determinants: education and health care. But the entire concept behind these social determinants is that our health and well-being rest on many factors beyond our individual amount of money— including community resources like "neighborhood and built environment" and "social and community context."

All ethical issues have a universal quality on the level of theory and yet are contextual in their application and action. It is a fact that poverty in the U.S. is quite different from poverty in developing countries, where some of the basics like clean water, food, and shelter are lacking. But simply saying to those living below the U.S. poverty line, or those facing an impoverished retirement, "You are better off than the poor in developing countries," doesn't solve anyone's problems.

In fact, the worldwide move toward thinking of our collective future through the lens of social determinants is pointing us toward an entirely different approach to responding to poverty.

For example, the World Health Organization (WHO) tells us: "Research shows that the social determinants can be more important than health care or lifestyle choices in influencing health." Remember our matrix from the last chapter? The WHO report is urging people to think far more broadly than individual success or failure as we try to plan for a better future. In fact, the WHO list doubles the U.S. basic five social determinants into a list of 10 factors we should consider:

- Income and social protection
- Education
- Unemployment and job insecurity
- Working life conditions
- Food insecurity
- Housing, basic amenities, and the environment
- Early childhood development
- Social inclusion and non-discrimination
- Structural conflict
- Access to affordable health services of decent quality

If we take those 10 seriously, then we begin to realize how cruel it is to simply dismiss people who seem to be failing in *The Game of Life* by telling them: Take responsibility!

And that's also why I'm not interested in making you feel sorry. I want you to think with me—to think together—in new ways.

Ethics—a very brief framework

Hopefully, if I have done my job so far, you are starting to see that there may be more to retirement income than you or I originally thought. We thought that you worked until you were 65, retired, enjoyed your remaining days with family and friends—and that was it.

But to call this the most pressing hidden ethical crisis facing us today, well, you may still be unconvinced. So, let's think about: What constitutes a moral crisis? Is this truly an ethical problem?

This is often debated, but it is important to land on some sort of definition that can be agreed upon. In some ways, it can be easier when the issue ties directly to concerns like race and gender equality. Marginalized communities are often a focus of moral concern. Sometimes, we can see a clear dynamic of a majority group actively pitted against a minority group. Other times, the problem is more subtle.

My proposal is that we face an ethical problem when a person or group, without just cause, is denied a freedom or a benefit that they need and deserve by another person, group, or system.

So, let's be clear: Keeping a huge number of people out of poverty is a universal ethical good. The moral value of keeping people out of poverty goes beyond any religious or ethical worldview.

Obviously, poverty has been a part of human experience for thousands of years. Even the classic competing economic systems of the 20th century—capitalism, socialism, and communism—agree on their central aim of creating prosperity and easing poverty. This is not to say that all economic systems are equal in their results, since history shows that some economic philosophies actually create and worsen poverty regardless of their intent.

I come from a Christian tradition that teaches concern for the poor. So does Judaism, Islam, Buddhism, and all of the world's great faith traditions. Even major atheist and secularist thinkers hope to ease the world's poverty as I have pointed out in an earlier chapter. This is a human imperative that crosses all social, religious, and political structures.

Poverty does something to the humanity of those experiencing it. No matter the context, poverty pushes people toward a subhuman condition where they cannot flourish and thrive. The world's admirable religions and philosophies encourage the elevation of all of us rather than the putting down of anyone's human dignity.

The worst moments in human history have occurred when people deny the basic moral and ethical value of others. I encountered this in 2007-8 while working with a group of political refugees on my staff who had fled from the former Yugoslavia. I will never forget a staff member telling me about military forces murdering their family while they were hiding in a box in the next room.

Poverty can be lethal as well. And allowing poverty to grow unchecked erodes the moral and ethical values of our communities. Those items on the lists of social determinants are not exclusive of each other. They are interwoven. Poverty creates food insecurity. Food insecurity creates malnutrition. Malnutrition reduces physical and mental capacities. Poverty bears bad fruit, for individuals, families, and society.

Many people have concluded that money is a necessary evil at best. As much as we want money—we instinctively sense that there are moral ills associated with money. It's no surprise that most Americans list money as their number one anxiety. But I want to encourage you to move beyond thinking of money as intrinsically good or evil.

Part of us knows that money is just a tool. Like a hammer can be used to both knock down walls and build them—we know money can do both. That leads to an even more challenging question: Have we been using the wrong measuring stick for American success? What if we did not judge our nation's success based on the wealth of a few, but the wealth of us all?

We are living right now in the midst of a deep ethical question about the growing divide between the wealthy few and the not-wealthy rest of us. I live in California, for better or worse. Depending on the way you measure it, California accounts for almost 20% of the U.S. economy, and it would be the 5th largest economy in the world if it were an independent nation. Yet we have places like Silicon Valley, the birthplace of the modern world, and nearby San Francisco with some of the nation's most expensive real estate next to a growing number of people without homes.

If Los Angeles, closer to where I live, were an independent nation, it would be in the top 20 of the world's largest economies—and yet we seem to have no ability to aid those without homes or to successfully manage our foster care situation.

So, in California, are "we" successful? Perhaps, on some metrics.

Did we do what was right and best for everyone? Certainly not.

When I evaluate what we have done and continue to do in the economic life of this nation, I do not believe we can say that it has been good for the long-term benefit of the majority of people in the United States. Is this our greatest achievement, putting all the wealth in the hands of 5% of all our citizens while the rest end up moving closer and closer to poverty?

Perhaps we are living through a cautionary tale—we may be headed towards the exact systems that led people to leave Europe and colonize America in the first place.

Taking this to heart

As a result of working on this project, I realize that I have not been as aware of poverty's consequences on individuals and society as I should have been. I must admit that one reason is: I never have considered myself poor. Even during a 10-month stretch of having no job while living in one of the most expensive places in the U.S., I never was without food, shelter, clothing, or other basic needs.

Perhaps I'm describing your experience? You and your family may never have wrestled with real poverty. What alarms me about this research I have been conducting is that there are so many of our neighbors across America who are close to poverty levels. Then, beyond that tragedy, a friend one day challenged me:

"What about the millions *already* living in poverty?"

I had no words. I sat there and nodded my head to convey that I understood this was a real problem. Saying something like, "Yeah, I know. It's not good," doesn't quite do justice to this ethical crisis we share.

Beyond moral concerns, we are truly all in this together. Even if you are relatively wealthy, the long-term stability of the economic system is threatened when the impoverished population explodes. Two things start to happen that can unravel the entire system, and they are simply history repeating itself in new and different ways.

The first is that people no longer want or can afford what we are offering across our economy. Here's a personal example: In my desk I have approximately $300,000 in the form of rare and valuable sports cards. Yes, I keep $300,000 in my desk drawer. From another perspective, I keep a lot of small pieces of paper with pictures on them that no one wants to buy. Both are true and in the realm of money and value, the fact that no one is buying them is an even more important truth, because that is the real determiner of value. My fear is that we are doing this on a large scale with the overall American economic system. The two biggest markets where I see this potential living are the real-estate market and the stock market. When people stop buying, the whole system starts to devalue.

A long time ago, when I managed Starbucks locations in my early 20s, occasionally, we would have a customer threaten that they were no longer going to come to Starbucks. Their implication was that this was somehow going to hurt Starbucks in a meaningful way. It was laughable to think that one person protesting and keeping their $5 from Starbucks was going to hurt the company. Now, I made sure that we ran great locations and weren't intentionally driving customers away. But I also know that Starbucks serves some 70 million people every day. Even if 10% never come back, that still leaves 63 million people coming every day. Any single person's decision to not buy their coffee from Starbucks again is inconsequential.

But what happens if we are continually making a higher and higher percentage of the population unable to partake in what we are selling? This is the downward cycle we have already entered. Prices and values can go down and so can the stock prices of these things that people own. That only complicates things because so many have their own worth tied up in those areas, like stocks.

The second place this downward spiral reveals itself is in the housing market. Real estate has long been an essential part of the American Dream. Please, hear me clearly when I say that home ownership is not bad—it just is not what it was for previous generations. The new generations are changing the game. What happens to the wealth that people have tied up in their homes if the next generation is unable to afford to buy such homes? What will the value of homes be then?

Are we already there?

I think that the distribution of wealth across America is now so imbalanced that we are at an inflection point when the rate of change in our basic economic assumptions can speed up at an alarming rate.

We are facing the declining ability of most of us here in the United States to be able to provide for our economic needs in accordance with the most basic of human needs and rights.

This is the great socioeconomic fork in the road.

Cynicism will not help.

Opting out of this ethical and moral dilemma is not possible, because we all are in this vortex together.

10

The Trifecta

Before we turn toward solutions, there is one more major challenge we need to consider. So far, we have been looking at the future poor mainly in these terms:

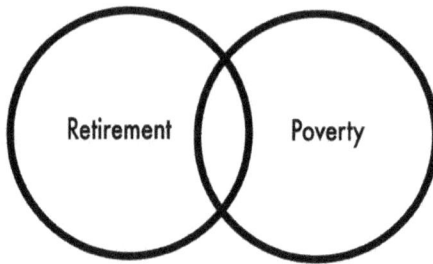

Retirement   Poverty

However, as we search for solutions, we are not all able to approach this looming reality with clear minds. The trifecta we are facing includes "mental illness," which I am using to describe either forms of mental disorder or cognitive decline that are more likely to occur as we age. This will not surprise people who live in major metropolitan areas where we are more likely to see the immediate and devastating effects of this correlation. Those of us who have interacted with people who have been living without homes for a long period of time understand this related challenge. Sometimes mental illness contributes to a personal crisis—and sometimes a mental toll results from dire poverty. They feed each other, reinforce each other, and strengthen each other.

To fully understand the future poor, we need to think in these terms:

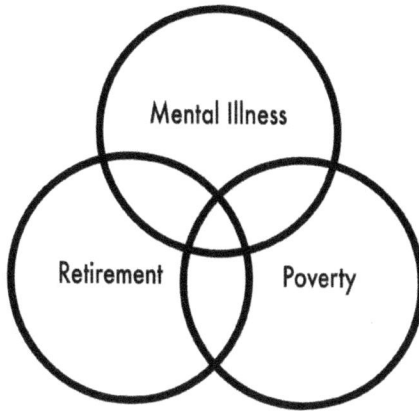

Over the years, I have had the privilege of working alongside many people in the Los Angeles area who are experts on this dynamic. This situation in Los Angeles is about as complex as a human and moral situation can get. We wrestle with so many questions: Is the solution a house and job? Maybe if our communities had adequate psychiatric help? Perhaps if the "system" hadn't let so many people down?

The answer will require a significant movement in all of those areas. Poverty and mental health are inextricably linked—always has been and probably always will be.

My friends who work in the foster care system here in Los Angeles see this from the vantage point of keeping the next generation from entering this cycle. Los Angeles has the largest number of youths in the foster care and state care system in the country. One person working in this system pointed out to me that these kids are "the future homeless." It was not an offhand comment. No, it was the stark reality of what they were seeing and trying to prevent every day.

Those who are at the other end of life in their 70s, 80s or 90s often grapple with diminished mental capacity. In 2020, National Institute on Aging data was compiled in "the first comprehensive analysis of the burden of cognitive impairment for the U.S. population age 50 and older."

The publicly reported study concluded:

Approximately two out of three Americans experience some level of cognitive impairment at an average age of approximately 70 years. For dementia, lifetime risk for women (men) is 37% (24%) and mean age at onset 83 (79) years. Women can expect to live 4.2 years with mild impairment and 3.2 with dementia, men 3.5 and 1.8 years. A critical finding is that for the most advantaged groups, cognitive impairment is both delayed and compressed toward the very end of life. In contrast, despite the shorter lives of disadvantaged subgroups, they experience a younger age of onset, higher lifetime risk, and more years cognitively impaired.

More than likely, you've had family or a close friend's aging family members experience some kind of mental decline. Unfortunately, for those involved, the financial ramifications tend toward the downside, increasing the likelihood of poverty.

But there is another aspect of retirement that relates to poverty and mental decline. Recent research is showing that retirement can contribute to mental disorders in ways we haven't considered before. A 2019 study by Jan van Ours and Matteo Picchio concluded that single men especially are prone to declining mental health, likely because as a population they become more isolated. This makes sense in light of social determinants research. Interestingly, van Ours and Picchio found that women and men with partners did not experience this same trend.

Clearly, there is something wrong with our idealized visions of individual retirement. And, again, I must admit: More than once I have looked at people and silently thought: You got what you asked for. Surely you've had similar thoughts when encountering some retirees. For us as a society, we have been on an individualistic mission for many years—and in many ways we are all getting what we asked for. What no one told us was: Becoming a completely free individual isn't all that wonderful!

People do not want to work forever. Yet people require the meaning and social connections that working affords them. This may well be the most undervalued aspect of work in our current day. Work provides us with social benefits far more mentally important than the paycheck we receive.

One study identified high-performing athletes who retired early because of their earnings—or because they aged out of their profession—essentially these individuals found themselves done with "work" before age 40. In many instances, a lack of purpose became a driver for the onset of depression. If they weren't competing for a championship, what were they doing? Many retirees find themselves in the same boat.

This connects to another series of studies about retirement that are important to consider. Isolated and sedentary lifestyles are correlated with the onset of depression and the acceleration of serious mental disorders like dementia. The World Health Organization's report on Mental Health of Older Adults tells us that a quarter of older people are affected by social isolation and loneliness—millions of people! Organizations, including our own National Aging Network and Area Agencies on Aging, report that isolation and exclusion are especially acute in many impoverished areas of the U.S.—both urban neighborhoods and rural parts of the country. In fact, Area Agencies on Aging regard isolation and exclusion as the most important factors to address in improving the well-being of a community.

Add to all that data the collective experience we all know so well from the global COVID pandemic. This drift toward increasing isolation is not healthy for us and contributes directly to the trifecta.

How can we solve this?

Oddly enough, the recommendations could easily be summarized into one simple statement, "Don't retire!" The primary recommendation that keeps popping up in lists of strategies to deal with these growing problems is: "Get a job!"

Of course, these recommendations are not exactly the opposite of retiring. What they are addressing is daily activity and interaction for individuals and greater participation in the larger community. Some recommendations are point blank: Get a job! But the list of solutions also includes actively volunteering, spending lots of time with family and friends, or moving into a retirement community. Bottom line: If you don't intentionally spend time with other people, you may wind up fast-tracking depression and mental illness.

For our purposes of looking to the future, the trifecta of retirement, poverty, and mental illness is a type of death spiral that does nobody good when layered together. This is why it is critical for us to begin making headway in delivering a new outcome for the last season of human life.

The Trust We Share

By now, if I have done my job, you have a picture of the challenge ahead. Retirement is less about beaches and margaritas than it is about worry and limited income.

I realize that I am flipping the arc of a cherished American narrative, but I have been laying the foundation for what I hope can be a new American story—perhaps a new American dream.

That re-envisioning of our future begins with new images that can stir us to action.

Let's start with the idea of "fiat currency." The phrase has gained a lot more traction in our ever-evolving financial ecosystem with the rise of cryptocurrencies, digital currencies, blockchains, and other new technologies. What is "fiat" exactly? In Latin, it means "let it be done" and it refers to something embodied in a decree. Think of "speaking something into existence." One common use is in the biblical tradition with the idea of God creating the world by his spoken word—by fiat.

Fiat currency goes much deeper than the current conversation around crypto. In fact, most major accepted currencies are really fiat currencies. The U.S. dollar (USD), euro, British pound, Japanese yen, and so on are all fiat currencies. For most of U.S. history, Americans theoretically were able to exchange their USD for an equal amount in gold, sometimes called "convertibility" and summed up as the "gold standard." Back in 1933, President Franklin Roosevelt began tackling the Great Depression by abandoning the "gold standard" and moving toward what today we call a fiat currency. However, it wasn't until 1971 that the U.S. ended convertibility.

Here's the key lesson I hope you will remember: It takes quite a bit of belief in something for it to have true value.

I think of this as "The Belief Bubble." Here's how it works. For our American currency to work in daily commercial transactions, it requires an *entity* (in this case, the U.S. government), the *people* (U.S. citizens), and the *fiat item* (USD). As long as all of those components work together and do their part, the dollar works. The *entity* makes and controls the *fiat item* so that it maintains its value and usefulness. The *fiat item* must stay valuable so that it can be used by *people* and the *entity* for its intended purpose of value and exchange for labor, goods, and services.

Should any of these parts not play their role, the bubble bursts. In terms of currency, we have seen this at various times in human history. When people lose faith in their government or when a totalitarian dictatorship overextends its reach, economic disruption is sure to follow. At times, a country's currency becomes worthless. This normally begins when the rest of the world sees it as having no value which quickly destabilizes the country, causing hyper-inflation, economic collapse, and more.

Today, millions of Americans are feeling this anxiety about our key civic and social structures. Take higher education for example. Today, people are questioning its value. Younger generations are weighing if the student loan debt they will incur is worth the economic outcome they are promised. For some, the cost/benefit analysis makes sense. But others are saying: "Nope!" We are seeing that kind of destabilization in many of our civic and social structures. And, yes, a crumbling faith in our fiat currency, the USD, can contribute to that destabilization as well.

So, let's look more closely at why our fiat currency works. The key to our currency's value is not just the way we use it, depend on it, and believe in it on a daily basis in our communities. No, the real power of the USD comes from the billions of people outside the U.S. who believe in it. When Iceland's currency is devalued, there is little impact on the world stage. In contrast, if the USD were to fall—or worse, fail—some level of global economic collapse would be imminent. This is not to say the USD is somehow superior or that those of us in America are better than others on the global stage. This is to illustrate how something that is made by decree and out of nothing—by fiat—can gain power and be believed in for the betterment of the world.

And therein lies the rub for our key civic and social structures and their roles in the looming crisis of the future poor. When we wake up each morning, we trust in the stability of the many institutions on which we will depend that day—from our faith that we can buy healthy food in our grocery stores—to our trust that emergency rooms and an entire health care system are available if we suddenly have a health crisis—to our trust that public safety forces are protecting us from crime. Do you see the principle at work in each example? The stability of these civic and social structures does not depend entirely on those working inside those institutions. Their stability depends on those outside these systems believing that they are real and valuable resources—and encouraging support for those institutions.

So, it's time for another thought experiment. Let's consider your attitudes toward what I described in Chapter 5 as "The 5 Social Pillars of Retirement"—family, religion, education, government, and corporations.

Do you feel like you are getting significant benefit from the following?

Rate them on a scale of 1 to 5. At the top of the scale is 5, meaning that you are benefiting a great deal and strongly believe in supporting that pillar. At the bottom is 1, meaning that you don't see much value in these institutions.

After you give each one your rating, go back and rate them based on what you're hearing from the people around you—family, friends, and co-workers.

- Family 1 2 3 4 5
- Religion 1 2 3 4 5
- Education 1 2 3 4 5
- Government 1 2 3 4 5
- Corporations 1 2 3 4 5

Without knowing you, I can probably guess within a pretty close range how you scored each item.

Family is a mixed bag depending on the family you come from—but I'm guessing you gave family a 4 or maybe even the only 5 on the list. I'll admit, my hunch was informed by data that makes guessing accurately a lot easier. Pew research shows that "9-in-10 say they view [family] either as one of the most important things or as very important but not the most important thing." That finding crosses political lines as well.

Religion. This is where we probably go lower. Some people will rate it 3 or below. All of us are keenly aware that religious life has been in decline in this country. Some would say that decline is at the heart of many problems. Others would say the decline is a sign that religion needs reform. There is probably truth in both. What the majority do agree on is that religion is losing its influence, which is a sign that it is losing its perceived value.

Education. Your rating will depend on how much student loan debt you left college with and how valuable your degree has proven to be. So, probably a 2 or slightly higher depending on your age, how much higher education you had, and your political leanings. No one is happy to carry around tons of student debt, but national research shows a real mixed bag of opinions on K-12 and higher education.

Government was probably a 1, maybe a 2 if you have more faith than most people. With the exception of 2001 in the post 9/11 era, public trust in the federal government has been low. Prior to Watergate and Nixon, public trust was high in the 1950s and '60s. As of September 19, 2023, "Currently, fewer than 2-in-10 Americans say they trust the government in Washington to do what is right 'just about always' (1%) or 'most of the time' (15%)." Again, this makes the job of guessing your response a pretty safe bet.

Corporations were probably a 2 at best. Americans seem to love small businesses and see them as overall positive. "86% now say that small businesses are having a positive effect on the way things are going in the country." When it comes to large corporations, only 29% feel positive.

Compare your ratings on these five with the ratings you gave them based on what you're hearing from the people around you—and you've almost certainly got a mixed bag of positives and negatives. Those ratings also may sketch a picture of bubbles about to burst.

That's not surprising, given the deep polarization that Pew has charted in recent years and daily headlines proclaim. I asked you to try this thought experiment not to further depress you, but to remind us all that the future effectiveness of these pillars depends not just on what "they" are doing "inside" these institutions—but on our attitudes toward, our support for, and our ongoing interest in shaping them.

As a nation, we have the potential within each of these five to move toward creating abundance for all. And yet we have been playing individualistic games for so long that we may have forgotten our interdependence.

I want to reiterate how important it is that those on the "outside" find value in and seek out what each of these five offers for supporting us, our families, and our communities. What I hope you are beginning to understand is: If we move further and further away from seeing the five as a real benefit to our society—if we lose faith in these institutions—our retirement problem is compounded.

It is easy to be a cynic in our current world. You are holding a book with a bleak title: *The Future Poor*. In fact, you may have picked up this book only because of the promise you saw in the subtitle: *How families and communities can join together to survive the looming retirement crisis*.

So, now, let's explore more about the potential of what we can achieve together in rebuilding the abundance of our American community.

12

Facing the Fork in the Road

Our American social compact is coming apart at the seams. At this point, it's not enough to join the chorus of people storming the gates of our civic and social institutions, shouting: "Hey! Help us—like you used to support our parents and grandparents!"

No, the challenges we face are bigger than that. It also is foolish to think that simply saving more in some accounts will cure what we are facing.

If you have followed me on this journey, so far, then we are discovering together that there are several levels at which we must rethink retirement—especially for the betterment of the millions of us in the sub-50 generations.

About one year into my own research for this book, Adam Grant—an organizational psychologist and best-selling author—published *Think Again*. Not only did that book encourage me to explore and discard old assumptions about retirement, but Grant's thinking also energized my own efforts to encourage people to envision new solutions to this looming crisis. In *Think Again*, Grant wastes no time in getting to his thesis. Grant writes on page 2: "Intelligence is traditionally viewed as the ability to think and learn. Yet in a turbulent world, there's another set of cognitive skills that might matter more: the ability to rethink and unlearn." Nowhere is this more prevalent than the world of finance and retirement. It is as if Grant is channeling my all-time favorite philosopher Yoda and his profound statement to Luke Skywalker, "You must unlearn what you have learned."

Moving beyond "us" and "them"

Let's start with that image of "us" storming the gates of civic and social institutions, shouting: "Help us!"

What's wrong with that image? First, it's based on an image of "us" vs. "them"—when, in fact, millions of "us" are "them." A huge portion of our American population forms the ranks working inside those institutions. If we forget that essential truth, then we give up our agency to participate in and shape a new future—from inside as well as outside. We must claim a new vision of participation and begin to break down the distance we are feeling between "us" and "them." It is not going to work well if we don't. Grant writes, "Rethinking is not just an individual skill. It's a collective capability."

This makes sense, doesn't it? We all know that we are living in a rapidly changing social, cultural, and economic landscape in which notions of our identity and values are all in flux. Of course, this has been a normal process for each new American generation—so it should not come as a surprise that those of us among the millions of sub-50/sub-150 Americans are the new shapers of our nation's daily life. With each day's headlines we see the evidence of how much we are collectively changing our concepts of family, religion, education, government, and corporations.

You've seen these changes everywhere you look, haven't you? Changing family structures? New shapes and structures of family life are all around us, including within our own extended families. Changes in our notions of race and identity? The U.S. Census Bureau just announced new categories for the next nationwide count. Changes in religion? Pew Research now reports that, when asked to name their religious affiliation, more than 1 in 4 Americans say they reject all the traditional labels offered by the pollsters. As a result, they're often called "nones," but that just means a quarter of all Americans have moved beyond the traditional religious labels we used just a couple of decades ago.

Change is not only possible—it's the reality in which we live.

Most importantly—all around us, researchers and community leaders are redefining the definitions—and the goals—for a healthy, meaningful life. Just like Americans are redefining our terms for religion, social and civic institutions are redefining the very meaning of health and well-being using the social determinants of health that have emerged so powerfully in public planning. Remember the list we considered in Chapter 5? Here's a handy recap—

The U.S. Department of Health and Human Services subdivides the SDH into 5 factors:

- Economic stability
- Education access and quality
- Health care access and quality
- Neighborhood and built environment
- Social and community context

When these elements are fulfilled in harmony, we have health that transcends individual genetics and life circumstances. However, what seems to have happened over time is that many of our civic and social structures have tried to retreat from this larger vision of community life. This leads many of our institutions to blame each other for the crises we face—and add to the sense of conflict rather than cooperation.

Today, for example, many schools define their mission as educators, not as health care providers.

Some religious groups have opted out of their responsibility for their community's economic stability.

Some hospitals only "do" health care, not social and community services, especially as hospital budgets shrink nationwide and their expenses have to be trimmed.

You can probably add your own list of examples to these three. Feel free to jot them in the margins of this page.

These disconnects I am describing now are crucial to understand, because therein, I believe, lies both the core of the problems we face—and our potential solutions!

Let's ask ourselves: What if each of the five "pillars"—family, religion, education, government, and corporations—took seriously their roles in contributing to the five social determinants of health?

What you will read in the rest of this chapter could be described as "dreams"—but I will remind you of Walt Disney's wisdom: "All our dreams can come true, if we have the courage to pursue them."

What if ... educators expanded their vision?

Our problem right now is that the socioeconomic necessity of education is creating economic instability—vast oceans of student debt—for millions of Americans. What if higher education made a collective promise to students?

When you graduate, you will be able to attain financial stability.

Did that idea startle you? Are you wondering: What college or university could risk making such a pledge? But keep reading. For now, I'm only asking: What if ...

In fact, there are fairly easy steps schools could take to move in this direction. I have long advocated adding a greater emphasis on financial education at all levels of schooling. I echo a common refrain from Robert Kiyosaki, author of the bestseller *Rich Dad Poor Dad*. He describes the difference between the people who gain advanced education and learn nothing about money versus those who learn about money and may or may not have any formal education. My one-sentence summary is that "my rich dad learned about money while my poor dad learned information."

Financial literacy can radically shift our individual and corporate situation. Formal public/private education must be a place where money is taught and learned.

Given our current money crisis, we must make math and learning the basics about money a requirement. We do not ask students if they are interested in learning to read and write! We teach them these skills because we know their intrinsic usefulness. Adults who cannot read and write simply cannot function in a society dependent upon those skills. Financial literacy is just as necessary for adult success when living in a society dependent on money. A Columbia University study found that people who did not learn to read or write were more likely to have dementia later in life. Similarly, people with more education have a lower prevalence of dementia.

My concern is that those adults without financial literacy seem to be heading toward a "financial dementia."

Education is profoundly important in creating financial literacy because of its dual roles of academic and social development. Children's minds develop rapidly, and we know their learning abilities at young ages are far superior to those of adults. They are like sponges, which is why many countries teach multiple languages to younger children. The content we decide to teach them at an early age will have a lasting effect. Education's second power is that it is foundational for reinforcing social development. There are rules to follow for classroom order and there are unwritten relational rules that can only be learned through interaction. Learning how to negotiate with peers and superiors, and to problem-solve disagreements, is fundamental. We should be able to move the ball forward in financial literacy for children by helping them understand key aspects of the financial world they live in and how to be socialized around money.

The state of Florida recently became the first state to mandate and implement financial education as part of their curriculum. My hope is that this is the first domino of many to fall in order to bring this type of teaching to schools. But the question remains about what aspects of financial life we should teach children. I have yet to review any curriculum proposed by Florida, but I have a sense that there are some key overarching concepts that should be included.

A survey conducted by ValuePenguin and reported on by CNBC found that 63% of people do not understand how a 401(k) works. That is alarming given the 401k's prominence and how many Americans are solely relying on it. It is also not surprising since most people I have worked with do not quite understand employee sponsored plans, their basic mechanics, or what options they have within them. Retirement plans are definitely one key element for students to begin to understand so they can utilize them once available to them. While there can be complexity, we can teach them similarly to how we teach students how the branches of government work or how a bill becomes a law.

What if ... corporations provided investment advisors?

What if your place of employment offered access to a private investment advisor as part of their benefits? This advisor charges $5,000 for planning fees but you get that service as an employee benefit at no cost to you.

Would you be inclined to book a meeting with them?

Or, what if your 401(k) provider also provided basic legal needs like drafting a will or power of attorney document just by being enrolled in the plan?

What if before enrolling in your company plan, you met with a financial advisor that knew your situation and the investment options within the plan and helped you decide what would be best?

This isn't just a dream—it exists!

The first thing for corporations to consider is the role they have had in creating the future poor and their proper participation in solving it. "Corporate social responsibility" is a trendy buzz phrase now. Companies desire that we consumers see them as ethical, as having heart, and as doing things for the improvement of society. Most major corporations have been using their power and prominence to participate in certain social causes. When the country was in a heightened state of racial unrest during 2020–21 after a series of racially charged killings by police, many companies joined in the conversation within their employee ranks and in the broader society to fight racial injustice. Another key focus has been with the LGBTQ+ community in seeking to create awareness and participate in changing many injustices faced there.

Sure, some people are skeptical of the motives of large companies, but I prefer a stance of believing that they have a different power for change than we could do on our own. Again, this goes back to resources—and large companies have them.

Were a company to embrace the looming crisis of the future poor as part of social responsibility initiatives and see this as of the highest order, they could become a trendsetter and take social responsibility to the next level. As I have said, I believe this is the largest ethical crisis facing us, and yet to address it seriously could be to the potentially short-term financial detriment of the company. Yes, it's a radical idea for a company to ask, "How can we create economic stability for our employees and our customers?" But the long-term benefits for our families, communities, and nation could be huge.

One immediate step would be to sacrifice short-term profit for greater retirement contributions on behalf of employees. For a simple thought experiment on this, I thought of Apple. What impact could they have on their employees for a fraction of their funds? Apple made $100 billion in profit in 2022. Apple employs roughly 165,000 people. If they took 1% and gave it to their employee's retirement accounts, that would be $6,000 per person. $6,000 doesn't radically alter Apple's success or radically change the future poor scenario—but it certainly helps!

If you worked at Apple for 10 years and got a decent return, that is an extra $80,000. Let's go one step further on this thought experiment. Let's say Apple focused the entire 1% toward the bottom half of earners at Apple. Those employees would have almost $160,000 in retirement after 10 years. Do you believe Apple's talent pool and the number of people who would want to work for them would jump? I think we could make a pretty good case for that.

The profits for the Fortune 500 float between $1.5–2 trillion depending on the year. That's just the 500 companies that are on that list. What if the Fortune 500 committed 1% to aiding this situation? That's $15 billion. I understand that there are holes in this simple proposal, but I use it to illustrate how powerful corporate America can be in participating in the fight against poverty. The law requires most to provide group health care and access to retirement plans, which is a start. Many companies now provide education funding or reimbursement. While noble, these only begin to scratch the surface of being active participants in the social determinants of health.

One of the ideas that I have had for some time is companies hosting financial training by reputable firms to assist in the financial education of their employees. This could be more powerful than they realize. Yes, it potentially costs money to bring in a presenter. Sure, employees would take an hour or so out of their work week. Yet, financial anxiety is the number one concern of Americans. Would every business benefit from less anxious employees? Of course. Do many companies offer this type of benefit? Not yet. It is even as simple as having an advisor help with the investment selections the employee selects for a 401(k). Right now, far too many new hires fill in their paperwork with no professional guidance on their retirement plan—the thing they are probably most counting on for retirement.

From where I sit, corporations and businesses hold several keys to the kingdom, and these keys aren't solely in wages and benefits, though those are significant. Most people cite time and not enough assets as main reasons why they do not seek professional guidance. Employers have direct control over employees' time and can bring in professionals for a fraction of the cost—potentially no cost—thereby eliminating barriers to entry that many employees are feeling. Few advisors see this opportunity the way that I do. I see that millions of Americans are in need of financial guidance and aren't getting it.

Ultimately, I hope that the economic idea of stakeholder capitalism does prevail over our current system based on shareholder capitalism. The idea of stakeholder capitalism, which has been gaining influence since the 1980s, is that company decision-makers should consider the impact of their choices on all stakeholders, not only their shareholders. If this idea does prevail, think about how this will impact the employees' lives. What will this do to the environment? What would this do to for the economic stability of consumers?

What if ... government changed priorities?

Let's ask a couple of "what ifs" about our government—starting with: What if the government's only role was to create the following?

- Economic stability
- Health care access and quality
- Education access and quality
- Safe and healthy social and community context
- Safe and healthy neighborhood and built environment

Wait a minute! You may be thinking: That should not be a "what if" but the only things all levels of government should be concerned with, right? Who would argue against the value of these goals? Well, millions of us do argue about how to fulfill these goals. If you think carefully, you will see the potential conflicts: For example, economic stability can be jeopardized in the pursuit of education or health care—both heavily subsidized by tax dollars already. How can we resolve such conflicts?

Let's look at some of the proposals.

What if we tax the rich and corporations? We already do that, and they tend to pay a disproportionate amount of the total tax liability each year. For example, one *Forbes* article looked at IRS data from 2014 and found that almost 80% of individual tax revenue came from people making over $100,000. Could this be more? Certainly, but at what potential cost?

The "rich" and corporations are some of the most tax-efficient and tax-savvy operators and so there will always be ways around proposals to raise the tax rates. Increased taxation could be an example of removing the carrot of freedom, innovation, and progress on the grand scale and essentially penalizing our nation's most important achievements. It also fails to see the economic and social benefit that companies have in the fabric of our country. Tax dollars are one way of contributing, but so are jobs and wages. Walmart has over 2 million employees and Amazon has over 1.5 million. Those are almost 4 million jobs that have been created in a manner of a few decades. How these companies interact with these employees through pay and benefits is a huge part of our economy.

At the risk of sounding like I am coming from one side of the political aisle, I want to be clear that the incentive system must be built to benefit all—not just the top. However, taxes generally are seen by corporations as a cost and, when there are tax increases, prices go up to keep profits where they need to be in our overall economy. The consumer picks up the tab in most cases, only furthering the gap.

What if we have a universal basic income? This is another solution that sounds good, seems possible, but I believe is hard to achieve. How a project like this ever gets funded is beyond my ability to project. Second, there is a false correlation in the idea that higher income will meet everyone's needs. That has proven to be an uncontrollable variable that more income does not correct.

To be clear, what I'm arguing here is that it's too simplistic to look at wealthy individuals and capital-rich companies as piggy banks for the execution of social policy. No, we need to find ways to work cooperatively—as partners in the social well-being of the nation. Economic and tax policies should align with the ethical treatment of people and be part of an incentive structure so that our economy continues to be sustainable.

What if the government's primary concern moved from creating economic stability for corporations—and returned to fostering the health and well-being of all Americans? What if new policies were routinely evaluated for their impact on the social determinants of health? How will this proposed law create economic stability for our people? What about this particular policy would open up more access to education and health care? In what ways are we creating more valuable community relationships for people while providing the infrastructure to support that?

What if ... we rethought our 'social security'?

What if our social security was not exclusively outsourced to the government and to social insurance programs, but brought nearer to those we are most connected with in our faith communities and our family?

If we hope to make headway on a national crisis as big as the future poor, we need to make changes that draw on the relational weight of families and communities—and deep values of faith shared by the majority of people. Not everyone identifies with a faith or a faith community—at least 1 in 4 Americans now tell pollsters they do not have a religious affiliation. And, not everyone has a functioning family network surrounding them. But, most of us share some religious values and are familiar with the importance of our families in times of need. I am not alone in lifting up this idea. For example, turn back to Chapter 5 and reread the section on James Gustave Speth, an internationally known environmental activist who makes this argument even though he is a secularist himself.

So, let's try a thought experiment involving faith communities.

This idea struck me one Sunday while running operations for a sizable church in Los Angeles—several years before beginning my financial advising work. It was the first time I began to see things through the lens of economics as it related to relationships. A volunteer was talking with me about struggling to get a website built for their business. This is a common problem people have since most people are not design savvy or technically proficient enough to get a great website built.

Shortly after that conversation I was standing in the back of the theater we used for services looking out over the 500 people who had gathered that morning. That's when it struck me like a lightning bolt to the brain: We probably have those resources that she needs in this very auditorium!

It wasn't simply that this one person's need could easily be taken care of by someone only a few seats away. Soon I was asking myself: What if we have everything we need in this room of 500 people to live as a healthy, happy community? If we can't meet every need, how many of our needs could be met by this particular assembly of 500? What would the impact be if we spent some time and conversation figuring out what resources we could share with each other?

And, if our community made this a priority, might this new kind of congregational approach to relationships draw more people into our circle?

Of course, if you know a bit about American religious movements, you know that's an idea seriously explored by a number of faith traditions, including Shakers, Mennonites, Jews, and to a great extent by Mormons, Lutherans, and Catholics. A large number of major colleges, universities, hospitals, and social service institutions nationwide have their roots in such faith-based movements.

However, in this new millennium, much of that earlier cultural wisdom has been lost. The Shakers have all but vanished. Many Lutheran and Catholic institutions have moved toward secular nonprofit or corporate ownership.

Looking out over our 500, I wondered: Could we reclaim this vision that is as American as our founding principles? Especially if you care about your congregation—and millions of Americans do—think of this pitch to come visit your house of worship:

> Here is what we do here at *Money Church*: We help provide for medical needs, help pay for college, are actively supporting disadvantaged areas and social programs, provide a diverse group of people to form supportive friendships for every stage of life—and we will ensure your economic stability no matter what. Want to come check us out?

This may sound radical: Faith communities must begin talking about money from the perspective of economic philosophy and the practical skills of financial advisors as well as developing a worldview that makes money an ally and part of the natural order of the world. Historically, American religious movements had their greatest power when they took such a vision and values seriously.

What is needed first is an honest and positive relationship with money. In order to achieve that within our context, we could require our community and national leaders to include a sort of monetary policy in their convictions and communications. We need the sacrificial humility of leaders and our collective intellectual humility to venture into this territory that today is largely unknown in our country.

For those in the Christian tradition and the one I am most familiar with, I see a need to shift the way in which we speak about money. Jesus had a nuanced approach in his teachings on money. On one hand you have the understanding that money is needed to care for the poor—and for those who have larger amounts of money, their wealth may be a spiritual impediment. Jesus most often focused on the misuses of money and its particular power. "Money is the root of all evil" is often quoted as a substitute for the actual verse, "the love of money is a root for all sorts of evil."

My Greek scholar of a father provided me some insight into this passage. He made the astute observation that this biblical passage does not say "the root" but rather "a root." This is an important distinction. It is far easier to say money is evil than it is to accept a more nuanced lesson: I do not have a good relationship with money and I do not know how to utilize it properly for its intended purposes. This is key step toward convincing religious leaders that we do, indeed, need to talk about money beyond annual fundraising appeals to support the congregational budget.

Another possible hindrance to discussing money more openly within the religious sphere is a potential confusion between discussing financial values with the dispensing of financial advice. I hope that this book is helpful in changing the way you, as a reader, think about money—but I am steering clear of giving specific financial advice. The central theme of this book, I hope, can become a model as religious leaders think about sermons, homilies, and talks in small groups in their congregations.

What if ... we rethought our family relationships?

What if we just started talking more openly about money in our families?
What if we thought of money as another member of the family?

What if we have the opportunity, no matter how little or how much we have, for it to be a positive member of the system and contribute to well-being rather than be a source of anxiety?

These questions may sound strange to you—but as I have been talking with couples about money, I encourage them to see money as another spouse or partner. Many couples try to ignore questions about money and let money, in effect, become a negative partner in their relationships. So, starting to take money more seriously in our relationships is a way to begin dealing with these "negative partners." Or, reframing money as a positive partner can open up new possibilities in your family.

Talking more about money is also important for our children. Discuss with your children some of the economic issues and decisions that you are facing as you encounter them. Here are some starting points for such conversations:

- When buying groceries, discuss the budget you have set aside for food.
- If you write a check (a rarity in our day) walk your kids through how to do it, where the check goes, and how the money gets taken from your account.
- Buying a car is a good time to discuss what a loan is and how interest rates work.
- When you get your paycheck, walk through how taxes are taken out and money is saved in your 401(k).
- Bills—especially utility bills—are great opportunities to explain how money works and is used for the different things in life that are good and necessary.

If some of the above suggestions feel outside your wheelhouse, take some time to think through them and educate yourself on the flow of money within your own life. The hope in talking more about money is that generations will have a head start and an economic mindset that they will carry with them into adulthood. Many children are shocked when they become adults and are face to face with the economic reality of our world. The earlier they are face to face with it, the better, so that it won't be as threatening and foreign as they approach adulthood.

The second step in the process is to meet with a professional and learn more about the technical financial side of your life. The sub-50/sub-150 need to become more financially literate for the sake of themselves and the next generation. Most of us relate to a family physician, through some kind of health plan—and there are parallels in looking after your family's financial well-being. For many who take this initial step, this may require some humility to have your family financial life opened up to a professional; but I assure you, advisors are not out there with the intent to make you feel bad. A qualified financial advisor is there to help.

Then, consider an even tougher question: What if the most significant contribution a family can make in fixing the current situation is through actual financial resources?

This far and away requires the most humility and the greatest sacrifice. Parents are generally the income earners in the family system until children are of age to have a job. Most of us probably began our working years in our late teens or early 20s without much money in our pockets or a tiny bit of savings. Few people enter adulthood with any sort of financial foundation to build upon aside from starting where most start—with $0.

The majority of adults today, when seeing what a small financial savings from their parents could have done for them, have this mixed feeling of wishing it had been done for them—as well as empathy when we realize that most parents have no idea the potential of a small amount of savings very early in life.

So, let's take a look at kid-savings scenarios. The first is $50/month and the second is $100/month. I recognize that many may not be in a position to set aside either $50 or $100 a month, yet I would recommend people work to find a way!

Scenario 1: $50/month

Three kids invested in the same thing earning a 5% return over 60 years, which is not crazy or speculative.

Savings is $50/month

Rome: Parents save nothing during ages 0-20, the kid starts saving $50/month at age 20 until age 60

Dawson: Parents save $50/month until age 20 and the kid does not keep saving

Kate: Parents save $50/month until age 20 and kid keeps saving the $50/month

Account values at age 20

Rome: $0

Dawson: $19,839

Kate: $19,839

Account values at age 40

Rome: $19,838

Dawson: $52,638

Kate: $72,478

At age 60

Rome: $72,479

Dawson: $139,666

Kate: $212,150

At the time of writing this I am in my early 40s. I would love to be a 40-year-old with an extra $50,000-75,000 somewhere. That would be a significant boost to the majority of those living in the sub-50/sub-150.

This is the power of generational financial planning.

Scenario 2: Same kids, but the savings are $100/month

Rome: Parents save nothing, kid starts saving $100/month at age 20 until age 60

Dawson: Parents save $100/month until age 20 and kid does not keep saving

Kate: Parents save $100/month until age 20 and kid keeps saving the $100/month

At age 20

Rome: $0

Dawson: $39,679

Kate: $39,679

At age 40

Rome: $39,679

Dawson: $105,280

Kate: $144,959

At age 60

Rome: $144,959

Dawson: $279,339

Kate: $424,300

Any financial professional, using a number of different financial products or accounts, can help establish these savings vehicles for kids.

In doing kid-planning with various parents, I run across several different mistaken beliefs and misunderstandings. One myth we commonly hear is that parents need to have their financial situation in order before helping their children. This analogy is like the advice we hear when flying: Put on your own oxygen mask before helping others. It makes sense on flights, and most of us think it makes sense with money.

However, here are two things to consider that make the analogy obsolete in financial terms. First, financial moves don't have to be in sequence but can be done simultaneously. The second problem with the flying analogy is that if you delay planning for kids until your situation is resolved, you rob the child of the most important aspect of money-growth: time.

If you take any lessons from this book, please remember this one: *Time* is the greatest variable for all things financial.

Another common rationale we hear is that kids will have to figure it out like their parents did—and related to that is the assumption that it is not good to give a kid that much money. There is the occasional anecdote of a kid squandering everything. But a lot of these rationales for delay rest on the assumption that our world is moving toward greater opportunities with each new generation. In fact, the whole point of this book is to challenge that assumption. Then, we need to ask ourselves: Do we really want to set up our next generation to struggle? Is that the best parenting strategy in an era of the future poor?

What if you don't have kids?

The definitions of family, friends, and relationships have evolved quite a lot during our lifetime and, in many ways, for the better. Millions of Americans don't have biological children. But, no matter what your age and familial situation, we need to remember that there is a next generation coming up behind us—including members of our extended families, friends, neighbors, and other people we care about in our communities.

If you're in this situation, ask this question: Do you care for younger people in your larger family, neighborhood, congregation, nonprofit, school, or community? If so, you could choose to participate in their financial foundation. Many accounts allow contributions and participation from all people, not just immediate family. Often, college funding accounts are a great way to participate.

A pleasant surprise

What I did not expect when I began researching this book was how much our looming crisis reminds us of the timeless value of "family," however we each define that today.

Family, in the broad sense, has an enormous socioeconomic potential to help us meet the essential social determinants of health. Family represents the deepest voluntary network of relationships most of us will ever experience. Another way to think about this is that the determinants show us that some form of family is essential for well-being and longevity.

What has been missing for most of us is a serious awareness, and family discussion, of the economic aspects of our lives. In fact, it actually may feel easier to just resign yourself to being poor in the future rather than to proactively begin talking about your economic life with your family. Yet, the potential benefits in opening up this discussion are so clear and powerful! You may find huge relief in ways that your family might decide to share resources in the future. But the process has to start with open discussion among ourselves as well as seeking professional assistance just as we already understand that we need a family doctor. Daring to ask the kinds of questions I am raising in these chapters with those you love may turn out to be a turning point in your own life's journey.

We really do need each other, now more than ever.

13

Redefining Our Mission

Much of the problem I am outlining in this book centers on the idea that we still are hoping to achieve the old paradigm of retiring at the age of 65.

But let's face it: That nostalgic vision just won't work for millions of us.

You may be saying: "So, am I going to have to work for the rest of my life?"

"Yes! Isn't that great!?" I could reply.

At that point, you might simply throw this book on the floor in disgust. And I get that! No one is thrilled at the idea of working until our last breath—including me, even though I have grown a lot more comfortable with the idea as I have been writing this book.

What I am saying to you is:

"Let's move on to something new and better. Are you in?"

A new mission

One of my favorite movies growing up was *Apollo 13* with Tom Hanks, Kevin Bacon, and other Hollywood heavyweights. It chronicles the Apollo 13 mission to land on the moon in 1970. After an oxygen tank ruptured in space, the mission was aborted. It had to be. "Houston, we have a problem." To continue to try for a moon landing would have been foolish. All focus went to doing everything possible to bring the crew safely back to Earth. That was now the mission.

The 1995 movie depicts the events that occurred in space and back here on Earth. In short, the disaster in space caused everyone to throw out a host of old assumptions and do a collective rethinking for the survival of the astronauts. One of my favorite parts in the movie centered on a growing issue. The Apollo 13 mission had a CO_2 and oxygen problem—something quite important when you are in outer space. CO_2 inside the ship was rising, causing a toxic situation on top of all that had occurred. Their CO_2 worked in one module and did not work in another. Why, you ask? The movie depicts that one was square and the other one was a circle—a serious problem that was later corrected by NASA.

A team, back here on Earth, took a pile of supplies that the crew had available to them and began to work on making a square peg fit in a round hole. They managed to find a way to make the incompatible parts work and bring the team home safe.

Our situation is not so different. We need a new mission and we have mismatched supplies. Luckily, we are not orbiting the moon with 1970s technology, fighting for our survival. We are flying through space here on Earth with 1970s financial accounts, fighting for our survival.

With Apollo 13, necessity required a shift of vision and mission. We are in the same spot, but how do we go about unseating such an entrenched idea as retiring at 65?

Most of you might be thinking about the idea of retirement differently now. It costs a lot more and is way more complicated than you originally thought it was. What we have not been given is a better and widely shared vision for the future than the one we currently have of stopping work at 65.

But, what if we can envision a new mission—a mission that does something beneficial for us all?

What could that be?

Well, one simple answer is: not retirement.

With that vision, I want us to adopt it as a choice and not because you can't retire. I may be the only licensed investment advisor saying this right now, while everyone else is still focused on retirement planning and making something fit that clearly doesn't. Ellen Langer, Harvard professor of psychology and best-selling author, writes that "without psychotherapy or a crisis as motivation, the past is rarely recategorized." Time will tell. But, I do have a good feeling about this new vision of "Not Retirement" as we face this crisis.

You may have to work past the age of 65, but that's OK! In fact, it may be one of the best things for you socially and economically. This is not to say that you will be slaving away at a job you don't like until you die. But rather, we should be rethinking why we should have to retire at any particular age—and whether retirement is good for us. As I mentioned earlier, the studies recommend that we keep working, which helps with our income and, in many cases, may keep some mental and physical challenges at bay.

Think about two people in their 90s, Warren Buffett and William Shatner. They could "retire" in the traditional sense, but have chosen to stay active. Sure, they are not as spry as they were 20 years ago, but they certainly aren't the stereotypical picture of frail seniors. While we might not be like those two, there is wisdom in considering how we approach our senior years in a way that is helpful to us.

While writing this I may have found one of my new heroes. My phone pointed me toward a CNBC article with the title "102-year-old still works 3 days a week at the resort she co-founded in 1940: Her best advice for a long, happy career." Deborah Szekely is the focus of the article—and many other features as I soon would find out. It is true: She works 3 full days at her business and is 102 years old. She also is highly involved in philanthropy and does public speaking. In a feature by *Woman's World*, in addition to working, Szekely points to the importance of social connections, saying "friends are key," and that "life is movement, death is not movement—very simple."

I have been building the case that the idea of "retirement" is quite different than it was before and so we need to approach it differently. Approaching it with the notion that this process works the same way as before is a fool's errand for millions of Americans. If we do decide to replace the idea of exiting the workforce at 65—let us try to replace that with solutions that work to keep us healthy and reasonably happy.

Of course, that is easier said than done.

How do we replace our 'affection' for retirement?

The first problem we face is: Most of us like the idea of retirement! We've come to associate that, as we have read in the earlier chapters of this book, with freedom and fun. For years before retirement, we may dream about escaping that old villain: work!

But is that really the story? I do not think it is. So, let's dig deeper.

First question: How could a new vision replace the entrenched American dream of retirement at age 65?

Answer: We need to replace that dream with something we desire even more. One of the earliest advocates of this idea was the famous Scottish theologian and author Thomas Chalmers (1780-1847). In a short work called "The Expulsive Power of a New Affection," he argued that the only way we enthusiastically start to pursue something new is when a new affection "unseats" a current lesser affection. The major pursuits in our lives only change when something greater comes along to replace what we desired before.

Second question: If we could envision a new post-65 paradigm that did not involve quitting our current work, would most Americans go for it?

Once again, Pew Research provides some intriguing, myth-busting data. Despite popular stereotypes about work as a negative drag on our lives—Pew found that the vast majority—in fact, two-thirds—of workers 65 and older "say they are extremely or very satisfied with their job overall." So, the idea that seniors we meet in the workforce would rather be retired is a myth. Millions of seniors are working well past 65 because they enjoy their work and don't want to quit.

But there also are ominous findings in this Pew report. That overall satisfaction with our work drops among younger Americans to "55% of those 50 to 64, 51% of those 30 to 49, and 44% of those 18 to 29." In other words, while a majority of Americans seem ready to work past 65, millions of us—about half of sub-50 Americans—aren't so excited about that possibility.

The most obvious appeal of Not Retirement is that working provides income—and income solves a lot of potential issues we face now and will face in the future. Working for income is the cheapest solution to the future poor. Plus, while you continue to work, you are delaying your use of savings and other long-term assets your family has accumulated.

And, there's more! As we covered in a previous chapter, it is really good for your mental health to work, which is critically important in your overall social determinants of health. Once again, Pew's findings underline this intangible but very important aspect of the work we do. Across all ages, Pew found that "4-in-10 workers (39 percent) say their job or career is extremely or very important to their overall identity." And half of workers across all ages say their work is "enjoyable" and "fulfilling" most of the time.

To be clear, it is obvious that most of us eventually will need to move from the workplace because of our age, our ability, or our health. What I am suggesting here is that we need to find a more individually tailored and ethical way for those transitions to occur than what our current system provides.

Did you pay attention to that phrase "individually tailored"? That means we are exploring solutions here that can begin with choices we make individually—and, by extension, communally with our families and our closely related communities of friends, perhaps through our congregations and social groups in which we're active.

That preparation begins with financial knowledge and planning, which of course is the central theme of this book. But this shift in our assumptions about the future—our "affection" for the direction we choose at this fork in our road—is more about recognizing and adapting to the world in a whole host of ways. That could include simple advocacy for those who are close to you in your family and friendship circles.

All work toward remedying the future poor is good and welcomed!

Adaptation

The world we live in is dramatically different from the one where most of the financial advice we have been given (or not given) was born. We must be aware of this, mindful to see if what we are doing still makes sense.

Adaptation is one of the hallmarks of biological, social, and cultural progress. Those who clearly see the change coming lead us into the new age. Those who willingly join in the transition are better equipped to live in the new world. This is where the sub-50/sub-150 find themselves as we face the future poor. Those that do not adapt will struggle to survive.

A central truth about financial advice is that it tends to lag behind the economic adaptation that occurs. By the time such advice becomes mainstream, the world often has moved on. The economy of 1950–1980 created the financial advice offered in 1980–2010. The economy of 1980–2010 created the advice of today, but we are not living in 1980–2010. What about adapting financial advice based on what works today and where we are going rather than where we have been?

And that's where those of us who are sub-50s now can play a major role in recognizing what is unfolding and pushing now for adaptation that could pave the way for a better future for all of us.

Information

There is no doubt that the internet age—complete with smartphones and social media—has had life-altering effects, increasing fear and anxiety, especially in younger people. We now are living in a strange world of fake news, misinformation, and confirmation bias as algorithms continue to learn what we look at—and then send us more of the same. We are living in a perilously conflicted "public square."

While all of that is true, these powerful new connections also enable us to learn things that were once out of reach.

There is no subject, no skill, and no strategy that you cannot learn about today. This is true in the financial realm as well. No longer is the world of finance reserved only for the elite or the licensed or the suits in an office. That divide has been broken down. There is still technical knowledge and long experience that those of us with training possess, but now the barriers to learning about financial systems have been removed.

The Pixar movie *Ratatouille*, about a chef rat, tells us that "anyone can cook." Armed with that, Remy the rat pursues his love of food. Anyone can learn about financial products, investment strategies, and so on. The internet is full of wonderful resources. The next generation is armed with these online tools—and they are using them.

Over the past couple of years, I have been surprised by the number of people approaching me about financial concepts they are learning about on TikTok, Instagram, and YouTube. This makes me excited, but I want to throw in a word of caution as well. These platforms are giving people the ability to teach concepts, market financial ideas, and debunk some old financial myths we may have all learned along the way. Armed with this education, more and more young people are making financial moves early and often and generally being more active with their finances than any previous generation. The word of caution is that many of the strategies, whether it's day trading stocks, buying crypto, being your own bank, dealing with options and margin, or aggressive real estate investing, have a complexity that requires extensive knowledge and careful planning, and, in some cases, involve great amounts of risk. If you are interested, sure, learn all there is about these strategies with what is available to you—and seek out a professional to go deeper and help you relate these many options to your specific situation.

Ignorance is now more of a matter of choice, not so much because the information is unavailable, but because people often skip over the complex reading and careful hours of preparation in their pursuit of what seems like a great deal. While today's online learning environment does have lots of mistaken, misleading, and sometimes predatory options—it's also an astonishingly rich library now available at anyone's fingertips. More than 700,000 hours of content are uploaded to YouTube daily. If you've ever looked up how to fix a leaky faucet or how to cook a steak, you could look up how to save for retirement and start learning some things in bite-sized increments.

Individual abilities

"Talent stacking" is a helpful term to learn. The old idea of a rigid job description that puts a limit on your work contributions is gone. Businesses are quickly realizing that their work force has skills that go beyond the specific role they were hired for. Capitalizing on these new abilities increases productivity and employee well-being. Some companies even build in opportunities for people to think outside their role or work on a product or project.

This isn't just a chance phenomenon of finding someone particularly skilled in an area they did not anticipate. No, people are pursuing the expansion of their abilities in areas that interest them. This knowledge is beyond something that resembles a hobby. It is a genuine skill. In many cases, this can lead to professional certifications. No longer do you require an additional 4-year college degree for competence in a skill set. You can learn to code, do graphic design, be software certified, and so on with less time, ease of access, and more cost effectiveness than ever before.

Many of the old constraints have loosened or have gone away completely when it comes to individual ability. This has started to reshape the workplace, how work gets done, and the entire way people earn money.

Employers are rethinking their hiring models, job descriptions, and how they access the range of talents of their workforce. There are also higher levels of specialized training being offered or funded by employers to aid their team members' development, make people more marketable, and help contribute to broader success. All of this is part of the shifting economy of work.

Entrepreneurship, the gig economy, and side hustles

Working a single 40-hour job as your only source of income is rapidly becoming a thing of the past and I am so glad that it is! To be clear, I believe in traditional jobs, vocations, and careers. These are economically and culturally important concepts that have been the foundation for the sub-50/ sub-150. Some would even say that this is what America was built on.

The reality now, however, is that having a single 40-hour job contributes to situations where there is little distance between the cost of living and wages. There simply is no way to nickel and dime your way to saving enough. Most people can't get a second full-time, salaried job for a variety of reasons. Most employers would laugh at you if you requested for your pay to be doubled. If you are paid hourly, labor laws prevent you from being able to work two times more hours at your job. It simply isn't the right scenario for exponential earning or for lifelong work.

What has grown out of this need for more income is something that is more at the heart of an individualistic, capitalist democracy and that is the entrepreneurial spirit. In many ways it highlights some of the best aspects of the human will, spirit, and ingenuity. It can also be a high risk, high reward endeavor. Entrepreneurship is one of the keys to the new economic world but also a powerful part of the remedy of the future poor. It may prove to be one of the significant income sources for us as we age and shift the nature of work and create meaningful ways to work into older age.

Entrepreneurship is one area of life where you can exponentially increase your income and have money work differently and more in your favor. As we open up new options for earning, we free ourselves from a pay grid, salary structure, industry average of pay, and so on. Those are important and designed to cap wages for the sake of business viability and profit. This shift toward entrepreneurial pursuits can benefit traditional businesses as well. Businesses no longer need to rely completely on their hired staff as more and more work gets outsourced to qualified individuals. In some cases, you may be paying a premium for the contracted work, but this may well save you from the overall cost of hiring employees.

For example, someone that is proficient in a particular software or skill, or has a professional certification, can leverage these skills in more ways than ever before. An accountant, for example, can have a W2 job as an accountant for a business. They also could serve as the outsourced option for 10 small businesses that need part-time bookkeeping and tax help. The second option opens up the possibility of exponential income potential.

These are just some of the tools of the new economy and will be critical for the financial well-being of you, your family, your friends, and society at large. If you want to learn more about entrepreneurship, a great resource can be found in Step 8 of Nicole Lapin's book *Rich B-----*. While written for women specifically, Lapin, a former anchor at CNN and CNBC and an accredited investment fiduciary (AIF), explains thinking about the venture into entrepreneurship better than most. Her ideas include approaches like being "funemployed" as well as the pros, the cons, and if it is right for you.

A thought experiment that I have run with friends, clients, and colleagues is to ask the following question: What if planning to "not retire" actually creates the best situation for you to retire at some point? That is probably not something many financial advisors have talked to you about, but it has the potential to save you from sinking into the future poor.

Is it better to plan to continue to work in your later years and then be able to stop, or is it better to plan to stop working and find out you have to keep going?

In order to have this new vision of Not Retirement we need to have financial planning models and tools that help us achieve that goal. That is where we will turn next.

'The Art of Winning an Unfair Game'

One of the challenges and potentialities of living in an individualistic culture is that everything seems to rest on our shoulders. We have achieved some of the highest levels of individual expression, personal freedom, and a real sense of sovereignty in world history. With this comes the full weight of that responsibility.

"We are on our own—yay!"

And: "We are on our own—oh no!"

The more we assert individuality, the more our systems are inclined to oblige us and move further away from us. In the realm of money and financial matters, we have seen that to be the clear case. Yet, even in our individuality, we are keenly aware that we are not alone, that we are not free agents operating independently, and that we are bound to some communal structures that can help us to succeed. Each of us has a profound responsibility not just to ourselves but also to those we are connected to in society.

This is the "both-and" art of living within a democratic society where the individual is sovereign. Independent and dependent. Freedom and rules. Order and chaos. Yin and yang. It is this ebb and flow that has been at the heart of much pain and also what is so wonderful about living within an individualistic, capitalistic democracy.

As individuals, we have inherited a major financial crisis, perhaps one of the most challenging and ethically alarming in our history. And now, we also realize we have been willing participants in much of what has happened over the past 50 years. On one hand, we have not been forced to buy every new product. All of this leads to questions about balancing individual responsibility.

It is an entirely different exercise to look at data, financials, and structural issues than it is to personally call people to action for the sake of our own future, our families, and our communities. And, yes, I realize that many Americans, even a lot of sub-50/sub-150 folks, won't fall into the broad trends I am outlining in this book for a variety of individual reasons. But I am calling in this chapter on readers' consciences or moral or religious values—however you describe them—to think collectively about our future that will leave millions in poverty.

Moneyball

Let's start with some insights from Michael Lewis, the financial journalist who has written such bestsellers as *The Blind Side*, *The Big Short*, and *Moneyball*. *Moneyball*, published in 2003, is subtitled *The Art of Winning an Unfair Game*. *Moneyball* tracks the story of the Oakland Athletics (A's) of Major League Baseball (MLB), General Manager Billy Beane, and their unorthodox approach to scouting players and thinking about baseball. By Beane's side was Paul DePodesta, his assistant general manager. If you've seen the movie with Brad Pitt and Jonah Hill, then you know the story. If you've read the book, you know the longer and more complete story. If you're unfamiliar, here's a quick summary: MLB changed as the 1980s turned into the 1990s. Rich teams, like the New York Yankees and Boston Red Sox, started to pay a lot of money for the best baseball players. By the time the story of *Moneyball* kicked up around the year 2000, rich teams had four times greater salaries than poor teams like the Oakland A's. And yet, they were playing the same game of professional baseball with the same goals of winning games and championships.

This created a dilemma, not all that dissimilar to the one in this book. In fact, the story of the A's is a beautiful parallel to what happened to the American middle class over the exact same time. The gap between the rich and the rest radically grew. Beane and the A's made the bold move to stop playing the game like "the old baseball men" and do things differently. What they did was adopt the strategy of a baseball writer named Bill James and Sabermetrics. They used statistical analysis to figure out a way to get on base, score runs, win games, and do it with less-costly players. They tossed out all the old "wisdom" and went a new route.

Outside of *Moneyball*, I do not think anyone has captured this better than Ellen Langer. In her work *Mindfulness*, she articulates an idea known as "entrapment by category," where we fail to see potential other uses of an item because we have been trapped into thinking it is only one thing and could not be anything else. She goes on to say that "mindlessness sets in when we rely too rigidly on categories and distinctions created in the past." This was certainly true in baseball. It is also true in looking at the current state of the financial world.

Along with improving their chances of winning games, Beane and his crew showed us how a community of players can win in the aggregate. Lewis writes, "What begins as a failure of imagination ends as a market inefficiency. When you rule out a class of people to do a job because of their appearance you are less likely to find the best person for the job."

Lewis was referring to baseball players. I carry his observation into the variety of financial tools (players) we have available to us—along with my awareness that the sub-50/sub-150s must put a financial team on the field to "win." I've also learned from Lewis to think of the sub-50/sub-150 as a vast group of people who financial institutions have regarded with a tragic failure of imagination. How many sub-50/sub-150s hear from a financial advisor: "There's not a lot of money to invest or a lot of assets to manage, so we aren't going to work with you." That is unfortunate.

At any rate, it takes an incredible amount of imagination to rethink the almost $40 trillion industry called retirement accounts. I like those types of challenges and so I set out to reimagine what could work for the middle class and it isn't the wisdom of the financial industry's version of "old baseball men." We start by realizing that the sub-50/sub-150s simply can't save and invest their way out of the looming future poor. We need to think well beyond common financial tools, stocks and bonds. For example, common advice is that Wall Street works for everyone—but just look at the numbers: 89% of stocks are owned by 10% of people.

Let that sink in.

I echo what Andrea Longton, CFA (chartered financial analyst) writes in *The Social Justice Investor* when she says plainly, "Wall Street culture isn't working for us."

Wall Street matters more than we may know. You can read the book *Why Wall Street Matters* by William D. Cohan to understand how important it has been for the positive social and economic rise in America. And it is nowhere close to perfect. But let's keep thinking about what we can do as individuals since we currently are on our own and working toward a better socioeconomic reality.

Dollars are what you are after but not in the way you've been taught. More of them probably work better than less in almost every case—this certainly matters for retirement! But it's not dollars you really want—it is what those dollars can do for you in a complicated financial game such as ours. Again, think of the *Moneyball* lessons: Dollars buy players. Players score runs. Runs win the financial game of life.

Think about a few financial tools—because it is more important to think about the use of money rather than the accumulation of it. Longton has a particularly poignant chapter on "Reframing Returns" where "traditional investors define returns on the money made or lost on an investment, social justice investors define returns as sustainable financial earnings coupled with social justice advances." We need these additional reframes that go beyond the simple formula of up or down to begin to reframe what is really required financially.

- If you are in need of guaranteed income, do you want stock market volatility?
- If you are looking to buy a home soon, do you want your money in a 401 (k)?
- If you have $100,000 a year in long-term care expenses, do you want that from a tax-free account or a taxable one?
- If you want your money to grow and beat inflation, do you keep it in a checking account?
- If you are trying to maximize your Social Security (as we talked about earlier), do you want money coming in from taxable accounts that increases your taxes?
- If you pass away, do you want a Roth IRA or life insurance?

In financial planning, it is more efficient with limited resources to use multiple financial tools than to try to get one large bag of money. This also reduces your risk of financial problems down the road. One of the most famous investment managers Ray Dalio, who founded the world's largest hedge fund, talks about "the holy grail of investing." What he is describing is the way multiple noncorrelated assets reduce your risk and increase your profit. Sounds pretty good, but what are these noncorrelated assets? In the stock market world that might be different sectors, like technology and medicine. It could be investing in different countries. For your stock market portfolio, this is considered sound advice. But I want you to think beyond just the stocks and bonds world, because there is a bigger game at play.

Going back to the bullet point list above and thinking about the use of different financial tools is important. They all work in different ways and if you do not use them, you may not be as secure as you could be.

Let's look at some specific options.

Pooled resources

Much like the surprising insight I personally had, that family and faith were going to be central to course correction, I was surprised to come to the following conclusion about what I call "pooled resources." In short, these are financial products where you can voluntarily contract with others to get better value than you could get on your own. Think of it as a Costco membership but in your financial life. By getting your Costco membership you participate in the savings that Costco is able to negotiate for you to get you 48 rolls of toilet paper, 2 gallons of peanut butter, and the $1.50 hot dog and soda for cheaper than anywhere else.

Most of us are unaware of the reality that "pooled resources" is how we gain many of the financial advantages we enjoy. Here are four obligations you currently participate in that are pooled resources: taxes, Social Security, health insurance, and car insurance. The general premise of pooled resources is that when people pool their resources, the pool is able to provide more benefits and coverage for each person contributing than if you were to do it alone.

While I was writing this chapter, my youngest son broke his arm. We went to the ER, he had surgery, and got a cast. We recently got the bill and the cost of him falling was $12,000. For most families, that is at least 25% of their annual salary. For some, that is financially devastating. For those with health insurance, we breathe a sigh of relief. Two pooled resources covered this big bill so that I did not have to write a $12,000 check. First was my health insurance. Second was the fund of donations to the children's hospital that covers the difference.

When it comes to the broader landscape of finance, we seem to have lost this sense, especially those in the middle class. My theory is that we like to claim individual success for the times things are good, and we like to think it is a collective problem only when things go bad. This incongruence in our thinking has allowed us to forget what many hold dear, that pooled resources are king for those who are not living among the nation's top 1%.

Life insurance "planning"

There is no single greater way to have an influx of cash into a family system than through the power of life insurance. This is true with the most common life insurance type, known as term life insurance. For a generally low financial commitment, you offload the risk of your dying on to the insurance company for 10, 20, or 30 years. You pay fixed or increasing premiums every month for the duration of the term. At the end of that time, the potential benefits go away.

There are also several valuable forms of permanent life insurance plans that have different mechanics and more "living benefits" that are associated with them. Depending on the type of plan, you could get a range of benefits, including cash value growth, stock market participation, tax benefits, and early access to death benefits in cases of medical need and more.

Life insurance stands as the foundational element of all financial planning and yet we are quick to jump over it to focus on the "fun stuff" like investments. Those of us in the industry know that proper life insurance planning has the power to reshape the financial state for a family for generations, oftentimes more than any other investment can. According to the CFP board (Certified Financial Planner) 49% of their curriculum is based on risk management, insurance planning, retirement savings and income planning, and estate planning. All of these are key to avoiding the trap of the future poor, but we have to understand how to use these tools in our individual planning.

Our values are tragically skewed when it comes to insurance. I often wonder: Why are people more likely to insure their iPhone than their own life? If life insurance is so important and powerful, why don't people have it and use it?

The key distinction I think lies in life insurance purchasing versus life insurance planning. Neither one is bad because I never believe it is bad to have life insurance and I commend everyone that does. However, a purchasing mindset with life insurance can be quite different than approaching it with a planning mindset.

A purchasing mindset generally is guided by the adage "buy term and invest the difference." This sounds good in theory and is a catchy saying, but the heart of it is to get the least expensive thing you can buy to save some money. The single most important variable is low monthly cost. For many, this is the most important factor and is a wise approach when working within a limited budget. What can and does occur as a result of this approach is to shop online for the lowest cost and lowest barrier to entry. Many sites will pull up the pricing from a variety of carriers and sort out the lowest cost option for you.

But this misses what is really going on with all pooled resources, and to miss this is to misunderstand the financial reality that is afoot. With life insurance, you are voluntarily contracting with others to share risk, pool resources, grow money, and provide more benefits to the group than you could provide for yourself. It is not only the voluntarily contracting together that excites me in our community approach to our situation. It is that most of these companies, at least the really good ones, are the best money managers on the planet and can produce way more resources for you and others.

Here are three recommendations as you search: First, find a company that has been around for at least 100 years. This shows their general financial strength and experience. Second, find one on the Fortune 100 or Fortune 500 list. These companies have the resources to do things other companies cannot. This is especially important when looking at cash value accumulation. Third, I generally prefer companies that are "private" or "mutual" in their structure, not "public" or "publicly traded." Mutual means that the policy holders are the owners. Keep in mind: Having "mutual" in the name does not always mean they are! Publicly traded means that you can buy stock in the company and that they have shareholders. It's not always problematic, but publicly traded companies may prioritize shareholders over policy holders.

There are a handful of companies that fit the criteria and you generally won't find them on a search for the cheapest life insurance. That's because these venerable companies are playing a different financial game on your behalf than the individual game most are playing. What you will find is that they are in every part of the country and have experienced people ready to meet and plan the right strategy for you and your unique situation. They serve most every state and every geographical region and many work remotely, making it easier to plan from wherever. The other thing that is unique is that you pay no planning fees for the work the agent does. This will result in quality life insurance planning and coverage.

Every life insurance agent should bring up permanent insurance within the conversation. You may be the one who is opposed to whole life because a particular financial personality says it's bad. If you are able, set those assumptions aside and try to understand how it works, why it works, and why all of the banks use it. You may be surprised by what you find!

There are ways that cash value life insurance products like whole life have earned their criticism. Most of them are not built properly or won't achieve the objective that they originally claimed. Many providers do not offer the benefits that make them a worthy financial tool. Getting people out of less-than-ideal plans is a key part of what I do. I also want to equip you with the information you need to avoid a less than ideal plan.

If you wish to learn more, read *What Would the Rockefellers Do?* by Garrett Gunderson or *The And Asset* by Caleb Guilliams. If you are in the camp that is "anti-whole life," I'd encourage the work of Kim D.H. Butler and Jack Burns, *Busting the Life Insurance Lies*. Each of these valuable resources describe in different ways how life insurance has been used and continues to be used. More importantly, they help you identify good accounts from poorly made policies. These include high cash accumulation, low to no fees, favorable tax consideration, 100-plus years of dividend earning, and profitability.

Other pooled resources

The next two pooled resources are less popular compared to stocks and investment accounts. But I believe they have potential.

The first is an ancient financial product: annuities. The idea was that individuals needed future income and money managers were willing to pay them in exchange for current deposits. The money manager had capital for investments and the individual had the guaranteed income they so desperately needed. The other advantage to this arrangement was that the money manager could get you more income than you could on your own.

People are rediscovering annuities in new ways since they aren't all like they used to be. There are different kinds, and they have different features. Some of them provide people with much better income and more guarantees than ever before. They also are competitive in the retirement savings realm as well. All of this is to say that the more limited people's retirement resources are becoming, the more they are going to require guarantees as well as withdrawal rates that can beat the old 4% rule. The longer that we all live, the more we are going to need to make that money last. If you were thinking that your plan should last 20 years, you might want to more honestly focus on 30 years.

People have tended to think only in terms of a single nest egg and a single bag of money that they now use in retirement. That idea is starting to fade and give way to a new way of thinking that is looking more through a lens of exchange rate. Just like when you travel and have to trade dollars for the local currency, you pay an exchange rate given the value of the two items. With the single nest egg approach of old, you got a 1:1 exchange rate as you paid out of pocket for different things.

Today, people are starting to see that they can get better exchange rates on certain future expenses. Like the annuity mentioned above. If you must employ a safe withdrawal rate with $200,000, you are only able to exchange that nest egg for $8,000 a year using 4%. A solid insurance company may give you 8% for the rest of your life in exchange for that money. That is $16,000 a year. There are certainly different opinions about annuities and their place, but I see, with limited resources in the future, we will require some guaranteed money for life. While $16,000 a year is not that attractive, for a retiree who has limited resources, it may be the pooled resource solution that truly provides.

Gal Wettstein, senior research economist at Boston College's Center for Retirement Research, says, "When you compare people who have annuities to those who don't, there is a sense the ones with annuities are happier." This isn't just a feeling, but is backed by evidence. TIAA, a Fortune 100 company, summarizes the data by saying, "You'll be happier, live better, and be healthier." A Rand Corporation study found that people that have been retired 10 years or more and had annuitized income were 43% more likely to consider themselves "very satisfied" in retirement than those who did not have an annuity providing guaranteed income. They also note that those with an annuity were 39% less likely to report depressive symptoms—a reminder of the earlier chapter on the importance of mental health in our senior years.

Another of these places where people can get a potentially better exchange rate is through what is known as long-term care (LTC). This is a type of insurance product offered by a few providers that exchanges the dollars you put in now for multiple dollars in medical and care expenses in the future. The idea of LTC is that you are likely going to have this need when you are older, and that a potentially good way to save for that is through a well-structured plan. These policies are not all created equal. I strongly encourage you to meet with someone and ask many questions about how they work and if they are right for you. These plans are another pooled resource to be able to provide you more money, targeted at a crucial need, than you could have had on your own without the pooling done with other people.

If the person you trust with your finances is not a fan of any of the ideas I have offered here, I encourage you to speak with someone with a broader perspective on the larger financial world. Some people love these particular products. Other people do not. Likewise, some advisors are leery of the stock market; others love it. Talk to both sides to be informed by both.

I do not mention these products for any other reason than what I know to be the value of pooled resourcing and the increasing need for that on the horizon. If you are a parent and have multiple kids to drop off and pick up at school, you know the value of pooled resourcing. Many parents quickly work to find carpooling friends. This gets even more valuable for working parents or when you need to drop kids off in two places at the same time. Logistical challenges create the need to be resourceful in finding others to help meet our collective needs.

Hey, it works!

Guess what? This idea of diversifying your financial tools is not an idea I made up—it really represents the sound advice of a growing consensus in our profession. And it makes even more sense as we think about this strategy in parallel with models like *Moneyball*. Our focus moves from finding a single solution to creating a big pot of money—to finding a wide range of individual tools and resources to meet every situation we may face.

If the market is down, you have money elsewhere.

When the market is up, you have money there.

When you have a financial need before the age of 59½ —the age you can access money in retirement accounts—you have money available.

If you end up in the 70% of people who need long-term support and services, you do not have to liquidate your 401 (k) to cover it.

I hope you also are learning that you will need to consult with someone who knows all the complex rules and data about these tools to help you navigate this more diverse financial plan. But my intention in leading you through this book is that you will learn many of the questions to ask financial professionals. And, in taking that step, you also are pooling our collective knowledge—from my book to your growing awareness of these issues to resources you can find in your own community.

Moneyball works because our financial lives mirror the game of baseball. Baseball is particular and situational, which is why nine players are on the field and cover the entire playing area. Our financial lives are exactly the same in that situations arise in the game and depending on our team, we are equipped to handle it or we are out of position and give up extra base hits.

Sometimes, a financial player may look like they are doing nothing all game—just standing there in the outfield kicking grass and spitting sunflower seeds, while the pitcher is throwing 100 pitches and looks like they are active and doing a lot. All the balls in play go to the shortstop for routine outs. This could easily make you think the left fielder is worth nothing and you either think you don't need him or would do better with a different position. We can see the error in that thinking with baseball because we know the minute the ball is hit to left field you want and need a left fielder.

The same is true with all the varied financial products available. This is what I've been outlining so far. You may look at something and think, this hasn't been doing anything for me all game, but that is because the situation never demanded that player. Then the game of life hits something that way and that player is called into action—and the crowd goes wild.

It takes a team of players to win, and it takes the value of pooled resources to win.

In researching this book, one of the surprises was that the people most adept at pooling resources are often those in lower socioeconomic communities. A lower level of resources in general is a catalyst for a more communal approach to getting things done and making it through life day by day. This is true on a global scale and may be part of human nature. When things are hard, we team up. When we do not have enough on our own, we share—although one of the groups who has the least experience with pooling resources is the American middle class. So, if you are among those millions who have avoided the sharing of resources I am urging, then it's time to get started. One valuable first step, which also is recommended in most lists of social determinants of health, is regular involvement in a community group, nonprofit, or congregation.

Another step is to intentionally form your own advisory team. Making financial progress in today's economy requires a team with three key roles: first, a financial advisor to properly plan and position your money; second, an accountant well versed in the intricacies of tax law to get you into the most advantageous tax situation possible; and third, a trust and estate lawyer to help properly position and shelter all your legal assets and help them move generationally. Such an economic team will truly take your financial situation to the next level.

"Uh? Wait. There's a problem here," you say.

"What's that?" I reply, "You see how awesome they are, right? They're like the Avengers for your money. They have skills and knowledge based on years of work in these fields."

"The problem is: I can't afford an advisor, accountant, and lawyer," you say.

And therein lies an unfortunate barrier. What is often necessary for financial success and growth is reserved for those that can afford it and have access to it. For example, one investment firm essentially says on their commercials that, if you have $500,000 or more, their team of experts is ready to help. And the problem for millions of us: We don't have that kind of money!

It's easy to lump all financial professionals together as predatory—out to get your money. But here's the other side of that coin: We may want to find these services for free but we know people need to be paid for their work—the same way you and I want to be paid for your knowledge, skill, talent, and value.

To get you started, though, here are a few more ideas to consider, especially if you don't have deep pockets.

Just start!

Angela Duckworth's seminal work *Grit: The Power of Passion and Perseverance* begins with a chapter with the title "Showing Up." Showing up and starting is where grit and change begins.

Starting may be your biggest barrier.

When is the best time to start planning? Well, yesterday. Every day of delay in beginning to look seriously at this aspect of your future life means it will only be that much more challenging to change course. Nearly every financial advisor has some sort of "cost of waiting" chart to share.

Looking at this challenge in a more positive light: Time is the greatest ally you have! So, use each available day, month, and year ahead of you by meeting with a professional—an actual person—as soon as possible. And, yes, I know this is a hurdle that most people will never clear. Beyond our anxieties about not having enough money to start financial planning is the fear of revealing our existing financial status to a professional. No one wants to seek guidance only to come home with a fresh load of guilt. Then, there is the confusing forest of licenses and certifications and claims and pitches pouring forth from financial institutions.

So, let me also make a couple of basic suggestions:

I hope that this book equips you to approach a first visit with a lot of your own questions you need to ask a potential advisor. Perhaps, having read this book, you will be skeptical of single-path solutions and you will ask about more diversified approaches. You might ask about ways your plan represents pooling of resources. You might explore what a financial plan would look like if you did not quit working at 65. From this book, you should have a whole pocketful of questions to explore.

A couple of widely available options are major-brand banks and major-brand life insurance companies. Most major-brand bank branches now have staff members who can advise you without upfront fees. Don't overlook the possibility of talking with someone from a well-established life insurance company, using the tips I mentioned earlier. And remember, just because you schedule an initial meeting—you don't have to take the advice you are given and do not have to make any decisions at a first meeting.

But take action now—today. Make a call. Start the process. Ask lots of questions and be prepared to explore new ideas that we can weave together as individuals—and communities—to reshape our future together.

Hope

One of my favorite pieces of work on the topic of optimism comes from a financial book I recommend everyone read. In *The Psychology of Money* by Morgan Housel, there is a peculiar and poignant chapter about optimism and pessimism. He writes about the importance that these psychological dispositions have when approaching matters of money. I believe he is right when he says, "pessimism holds a special place in our hearts. Pessimism isn't just more common than optimism. It also sounds smarter."

If you've made it this far in this book, there is no doubt in my mind that the chord of pessimism has been struck—but I hope it is not the somber note that you walk away humming.

Housel is right that pessimism, quite simply, is easier. It's also easier for people to make short-term connections that lead them to be *against* something than it is to build strong neural connections around supporting a common good.

But, it's time for a thought experiment I think we all can share: Think about the last time you were up against a challenge at home, at work, or in the community—and someone around you had the audacity to be optimistic? Against all odds, they were cheering: "We got this! We can do this!" Who was that person whose irrational optimism turned things around? What did they say? How did they act?

That's one of the truths I hope you carry away from this book: Sure, pessimism has a whole lot going for it—but, when someone cares an awful lot, we can have our pessimism shift toward cooperative action.

And remember another truth, too: Common enemies bind us together. If a lot of us agree that we are facing this collective, generational challenge of the future poor—that can be a huge motivating force.

Recently, our family watched *Independence Day* once more—almost 30 years after the movie first appeared. Bill Pullman has and always will be my president. Near the end, when it seems "darkest before the dawn," Pullman gives a speech that lives in my heart.

> Good morning. In less than an hour, aircraft from here will join others from around the world—and you will be launching the largest aerial battle in the history of mankind. ... We can't be consumed by our petty differences anymore. We will be united in our common interests. Perhaps it's fate that today is the 4th of July, and you will once again be fighting for our freedom, not from tyranny, oppression, or persecution—but from annihilation. We're fighting for our right to live, to exist. And should we win the day, the 4th of July will no longer be known as an American holiday, but as the day when the world declared in one voice:
>
> 'We will not go quietly into the night! We will not vanish without a fight! We're going to live on! We're going to survive!'
>
> Today, we celebrate our Independence Day!

Chills! Pullman's speech takes our individual hopes, even our national hopes, and lifts them up as global hopes for survival.

Of course, that was a Hollywood production. What about us today?

Do you know what our common enemy is today? Money. The vast majority of Americans consider money to be their number one anxiety. While this is a problem and a real financial crisis is looming, we also could recognize this as an opportunity.

In my lifetime, September 11, 2001, gave America a common enemy. Perhaps you can remember where you were on that day. That morning my dad woke me up with the strangest of wake-up calls. "Get up, a plane ran into the World Trade Center!" Everyone was glued to their TVs that morning. At first, we were puzzled, while we watched one tower on fire. Then, we saw a plane fly directly into the second tower. Surreal would be an understatement. At the time, I lived in Richland, Washington, where plutonium for the atomic bombs used in World War II was processed. Now, it is one of the largest nuclear waste sites in the world. Down the street was Umatilla, one of the largest chemical weapons depots in the U.S. So, everyone went on high alert for obvious reasons after 9/11. For a while, Americans were able to accomplish things together that we would not have been able to achieve without this shared resolve to respond. Previous generations found that unity on December 7, 1941, following the bombing of Pearl Harbor and the U.S. entrance into WWII. Enemies have a way of igniting our survival and defense instincts and pairing us with others who are seeking the same protections. Survival is easier in teams. We are wired that way.

So how can money galvanize us into a national resolve to make major changes? How can money provide the shock we need? Are we talking about wealth redistribution? Wealth inequality between the top 1% and the rest of us? What about equal pay concepts? How about a minimum standard of wages?

While all those issues are worth considering, they do not represent the collective shock needed economically.

No, we need something else to set our eyes on and ask ourselves collectively, "What are we going to do about that?" We need something that does not break down across dividing lines. How about this challenge, then:

Millions of Americans—most of an entire generation—are heading toward poverty. How can we help them?

Widespread poverty is our common enemy. It spans income levels. It spans race, gender, and identity. Because of the potential of such a clearcut and widespread threat to motivate us toward collective action, I am full of hope and optimism that we will do something together.

Will we rise to meet the challenge?

"The hope that gritty people have has nothing to do with luck and everything to do with getting up again," Angela Duckworth argues in her book.

Can we do it again?

"Can" invites the examination of possibility. For us, the answer must be a hearty, "Yes!" Where there is a "yes" there is an opening for progress, hope, and movement.

"We" seeks to identify the participants. This is you and me. The wisdom rests on a growing global consensus that the social determinants of health—the forces and resources that contribute to health and well-being—involve all of us working together.

"Do" is the action and the energy required for any kind of change. This is no passive or ethereal work. It is tangible, practical, financial, and ethical. Action is required from everyone. We must begin to do the financial rethinking required to forge a new destination.

"It" identifies our goal. In our case, the "it" is keeping people from poverty. More profoundly put: Do we have the vision and will to keep our citizens from a dehumanizing existence when they reach their senior years? "It" is also adopting a new financial paradigm that looks for more cooperative financial efforts. Pooled resources. Shared financial lives. I hope that many will find that vision compelling.

"Again" is to remind us that there was a time that we once had much of the formula figured out. Among other historic, collective movements, we found a way to create social security for the retired. If we did it before, we can do it again. We have the ability to effect the change required. To do so will be a departure from current norms—but we should take strength in realizing that we have accomplished efforts of this magnitude before.

We once had a time where we had come further than any other society in creating avenues for those in their post-working years to not be subject to poverty. That must be seen for the feat that it was in the context of human history. I do not think we have let it slip away entirely, but we are close.

Finally, let's return to our impact filter from Chapter 2.

Here is what success looks like:

Success reshapes the current mindset about retirement to something conducive for human flourishing—socially, psychologically, and economically.

Here is why this project is so important:

The importance of this project is that millions of Americans are facing poverty. Lacking the resources needed for daily living is the most catastrophic thing to happen within any society—and yet our current systems will only drive more and more people toward poverty as they age.

Here is what we stand to gain if we succeed:

Financial stability and, hopefully, financial abundance, for more than just those of us who spearhead this movement as we create economic opportunities together. We stand to gain financial flourishing that expands and creates well-being for our family, friends, colleagues, and our broader community.

Here is what is at stake if we fail:

What is at stake if we fail is the ushering of more and more people from the middle class into a lower and lower socioeconomic situation as they age.

The late Gloria Jean Watson, under the pen name of bell hooks in *All About Love*, writes, "While careers and making money remain important agendas, they never take precedence over valuing and nurturing human life and well-being."

We cannot fail.

Thank you for taking this journey with me.

Connect with Jonathan Grimm

Thank you for reading *The Future Poor*. If you enjoyed this book, and think that others would find it helpful, please consider leaving a review on Amazon or on Goodreads.com.

If you'd like more information about Jonathan Grimm or about *The Future Poor*, please visit the book's website: TheFuturePoor.com.

Want to get book tour updates and financial news sent directly to your inbox? Subscribe to Jonathan's The Grimm News—bite sized articles about the things that matter for your financial life: TheFuturePoor.com/GrimmNews

What's Up With Money?! is a weekly podcast with Jonathan Grimm and Ryan Roope. In each episode they aim to fill the gap between 1980s financial advice and magic social media strategies to relieve your money anxiety and to help you out. What's Up With Money?! is available on Spotify and Apple Podcasts.

Contact Jonathan Grimm at thefuturepoor@gmail.com.

Inspiring Books

Two Envelopes
by Rusty Rosman

When you die, there are so many things your family and loved ones immediately need to know. With a unique blend of wisdom, humor and empathetic storytelling, Rusty Rosman delves into the often-avoided topic of death, offering readers a guide to navigate the complexities of both practical and emotional aspects of end-of-life planning. *Two Envelopes* is your voice, conveying your wishes regarding your death and your estate.

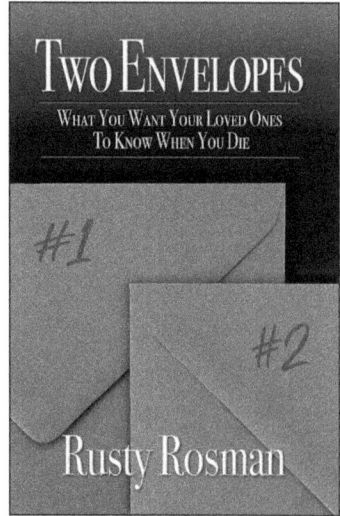

Now What? A Guide to the Gifts and Challenges of Aging
by The Detroit Area Agencies on Aging

"Now what?" Millions of us ask this question as we, or our parents or grandparents, suddenly face an age-related challenge. In this book, experts provide practical advice, including how to form a caregiving team, ensure home and online safety, maintain mobility and support independence. The book is written so that aging individuals, their families and caregivers can read it and find solutions together.

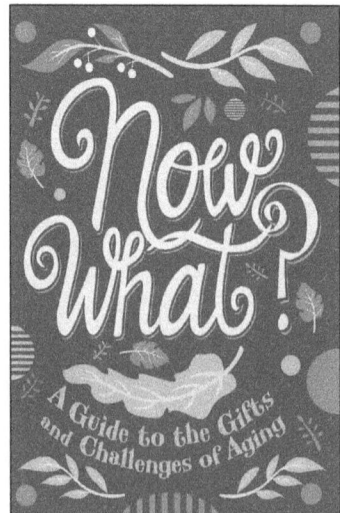

Inspiring Books

Introducing Christian Ethics
by Dr. David P. Gushee

What does it mean to be a Christian in today's turbulent world? Dr. David P. Gushee is an influential voice in American religious life as an ethicist, pastor, and activist. He's advocated on issues ranging from torture and climate change to truth in politics and LGBTQ inclusion. in this ambitious new book, Gushee sums up his many years of teaching and experience to provide a definitive, comprehensive vision of the Christian moral life.

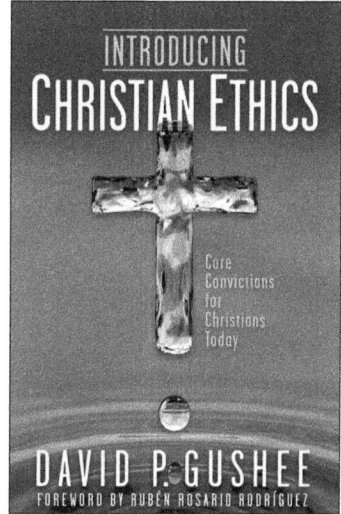

God Is Just Love
by Ken Whitt

How can people of faith foster love and resilience in our children while building sustainable, diverse communities? That's the big question Ken Whitt answers in light of the many threats looming in our world. Through wisdom he has gleaned from scientists, scholars and lots of real families, Ken shows how God's love is a hopeful compass in our lives. He encourages enjoying stories, songs and explorations of the natural world with children, and closes with "100 Things Families Can Do To Find Hope and Be Love."

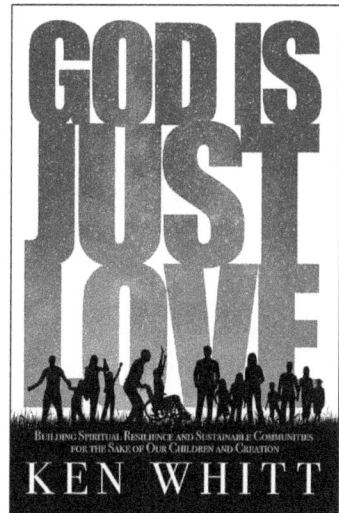

Inspiring Books

Tiny Homes in a Big City
by Reverend Faith Fowler

Tiny Homes In a Big City is the story of Cass Community Social Services, a Detroit based nonprofit that is in the process of building a neighborhood of 25 different Tiny Homes in the northwest part of the city. The homes are being built to allow extremely low-income individuals a way to eventually own their own homes. This is the only rent-then-own tiny home development in the United States.

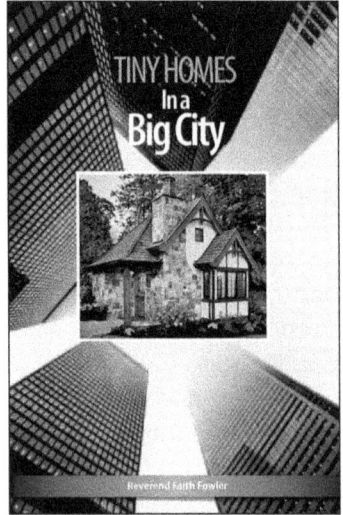

This Far By Faith
by Reverend Faith Fowler

Through reports nationwide, including the Wall Street Journal and TV news, Americans are discovering Faith Fowler's ideas for transforming lives in Detroit's Cass Corridor. Known for her deep faith and creative ideas, Faith serves as one of the city's leading pastors and as a nonprofit entrepreneur. As a co-founder of a wide array of Cass startups, Faith and her Cass community are turning one of the nation's most impoverished urban centers into a gold mine of talent and resources.

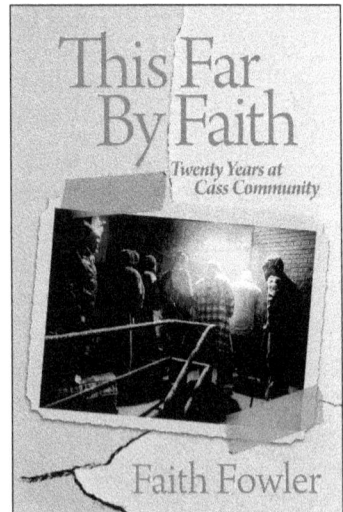

Inspiring Books

Hope for the City
by Jack Kresnak

This is the story of Father Bill Cunningham, Eleanor Josaitis and others who were drawn to the mission of Focus Hope. It is a captivating retelling of an English teacher who wore a Roman collar, rode a Harley-Davidson and marched with Dr. King across the Edmund Pettus bridge, a suburban mother of five who organized marriage enrichment events before she persuaded her husband to move into Detroit, the 1967 riot that exposed systemic racial inequality and the civil rights organization that evolved.

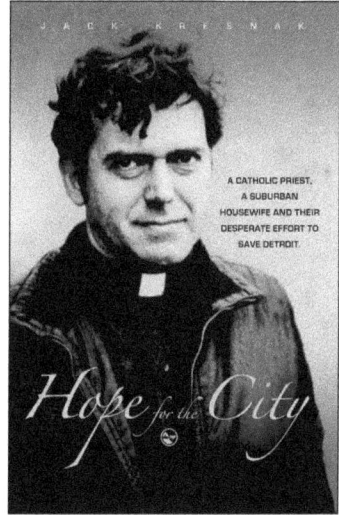

Critical Conversations as Leadership
by William Donohue, Ph.D.

Effective leaders are good communicators. Dr. William A. Donohue describes conversation as a card game called Card Talk. The key to successful business communication and interpersonal communication is to select the right Talk Cards in the right situations to accomplish your communication goals. Card Talk teaches communicators to think strategically and to think ahead of critical conversations and to not 'think behind' or reactively.

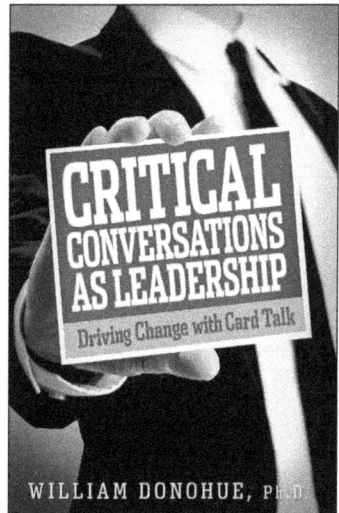

www.ingramcontent.com/pod-product-compliance
Lightning Source LLC
Chambersburg PA
CBHW021147090426
42740CB00008B/989